D1612272

CONTENTS

INTRODUCTION

'I have dreams of a red rose, and then of falling down a long flight of steps . . . '

Patient X, *Legion*

'David Lynch's good twin', is how *People* magazine once described William Peter Blatty, the leading exponent of contemporary theological thrillers, and a writer whose Oscar-winning work has been both hailed as 'deeply spiritual' by the *Catholic News* and condemned as satanic by the Reverend Billy Graham. Having made a name for himself in the sixties as a writer of comic novels and screenplays (he penned the Inspector Clouseau romp *A Shot in the Dark* and his prose was compared favorably with that of satirist S. J. Perelman), Blatty achieved international fame through more serious works such as *The Exorcist, The Ninth Configuration* and *Legion* which used popular fiction formats to address weighty philosophical issues surrounding the nature of good and evil, blending the surreal dreaminess of outlandish fantasy with the solid conviction of magical truths revealed.

Blatty's own obsession with 'magic', or more precisely with 'evidence of transcendence', has its roots in a youthful terror of death, and a desire to subdue the waking dream of obliteration which the author attributes to beleaguered mother Chris MacNeil in *The Exorcist*, but which is in fact entirely autobiographical. This blurring of the line between fact and fiction is a recurrent feature of Blatty's work; both *The Exorcist* and *Legion* were inspired by well-documented events, and both use extensive research to fuel their elaborate flights of fantasy. Even Blatty's most recent comic novel, *Demons Five, Exorcists Nothing,* has its roots in reality, using real-life incidental characters such as Florence Mahoney (who owned the Georgetown house which Blatty and director William Friedkin inadvertently made infamous) to produce a fictional reflection on the filming of *The Exorcist* and *The Exorcist III*.

Just as real events float in and out of Blatty's fiction, so ideas, phrases and characters cross-pollinate from book to screenplay to film, making all of Blatty's best work read like chapters in an ongoing debate. A casual, seemingly irrelevant exchange about lemon drops between the two priests, Father Dyer and Father Karras, dropped from the film of *The Exorcist*, resurfaces in *Legion* as a conversation between Father Dyer and Lieutenant Kinderman, subtly suggesting that the spirit of the deceased Karras now lives on in the unusual friendship between these two men. When the astronaut Cutshaw demands to know how God can allow innocent creatures to suffer in *The Ninth Configuration*, he must wait for Kinderman to suggest an answer at Karras' graveside in the final moments of *Legion* – and when that answer is itself excized from the recut movie of *Legion* that became *The Exorcist III*, it reappears in the mouth of the resurrected Father Karras in an epilogue to *The Exorcist* written twenty-five years after the movie was first completed.

While Patient X's dream of Karras' death in *Legion/Exorcist III* echoes the priest's guilty nightmare about his mother in *The Exorcist*, so Karras' dream reappears identically in Blatty's non-fiction work *I'll Tell Them I Remember You* as the author's own haunted vision of *his* dead mother. And throughout all of these works, the characters come back to a single rhetorical question posed variously by Colonel Kane, Father Dyer, Sprightly God and ultimately Blatty himself, namely: If all the evil in the world makes you believe in the devil, then how do you account for all the good?

For William Peter Blatty, the tangible evidence of a 'force of evil' is itself ironically a reaffirmation of the existence of divinity – evil is always the crucible of good, and the devil cannot but do God's bidding. Although he has been wrongly perceived as a purveyor of horror fiction, Blatty's novels and screenplays can more accurately be characterised as evangelical entertainment in which shocks provide the emotional charge while the intellect edges towards an acceptance of faith. This is the paradox that lies at the heart of both *The Exorcist* and *Legion* – the strange realization that die-hard sceptics Father Karras and Lieutenant Kinderman both ultimately long for manifestations of the supernatural because they would provide evidence that the world is more than just 'a homicide victim' in which 'our children suffer and our loved ones die.'

This is the key to understanding *The Exorcist* (both novel and film), whose positive message has often been overshadowed by its misleadingly terrifying reputation. In Blatty's story, an avowedly atheist actress, Chris MacNeil, turns to two Jesuit priests to free her daughter from what she has come to believe is demonic possession. While investigating the case, Father Karras comes face to face with undeniably paranormal phenomena which force him to address his own lack of faith, and which ultimately facilitate his salvation.

Although fictional, Blatty's narrative has its roots in real-life events reported in the *Washington Post* on 20 August 1949 under the eye-catching headline 'PRIEST FREES MT. RAINIER BOY REPORTED HELD IN DEVIL'S GRIP'. According to Bill Brinkley's front page story, a fourteen-year-old boy from a suburb of Maryland had become beset by poltergeist and severe behavioral disorders which had only desisted following a lengthy series of exorcisms. The boy's symptoms allegedly included uncontrollable rages and the mouthing of religious and sexual obscenities; a hideous transformation of voice and features; and the appearance on his skin of 'dermal brandings', bold red welts that seemed to form numbers, letters and on one occasion 'the image of a bat-like devil'. During the three-month period of the 'infestation', many observers also witnessed telekinetic phenomena, including the unassisted moving of a bedstand and a heavy armchair, and the levitation of a hospital nightstand.

As a freshman at the Jesuit-run Georgetown University, Blatty had taken a particular interest in this story, which seemed to him to present 'tangible evidence of transcendence'. Years later, he attempted to put together a non-fiction account of the case with the co-operation of the exorcist Father William Bowdern, but was refused permission by the Bishop of St Louis who had laid down strict instructions forbidding any publicity. Instead, Blatty wrote a fictional novel inspired by the Mount Rainier exorcism, but also drawing on other reported cases of possession, such as that involving a forty-year-old woman in Earling, Iowa, in 1928. Other sources included Frank Sheed's respected tome *Satan*, Traugott Oesterreich's *Possession* and Aldous Huxley's *The Devils of Loudun*, as well as Carl Jung's essay 'On the Psychology and Pathology of So-Called Occult Phenomena', which grippingly describes the case of a fifteen-year-old girl who manifested three different personalities, one of whom spoke a High German dialect unknown to the girl herself.

In all of these sources, claims of 'demonic possession' are

consistently balanced against more scientific solutions which describe even apparently supernatural phenomena such as telekinesis in the more down-to-earth terms of psychosomatic disorders. Whatever his own beliefs, Blatty was aware that as early as 1583, the Synod of Rheims was warning potential exorcists that 'lunatics often declare themselves to be possessed and tormented by the devil; and these people are nonetheless more in need of a doctor than an exorcist'. Thus, in fashioning his fictional tale of Regan MacNeil, the twelve-year-old child whose apparent demonic possession offers 'evidence of transcendence' to the priest of faltering faith, he retained throughout the possibility that her disorder may be hysterical rather than supernatural. This was an element which would prove particularly important to agnostic director William Friedkin when the time came to bring Blatty's startling tale to the screen.

Sold to Warner Bros as a movie while the novel was still at galley stage, Blatty's first screenplay for *The Exorcist* (published in *William Peter Blatty on The Exorcist from Novel to Film*) was, frankly, unfilmable. Utilizing an array of stylistic quirks including flashbacks, freeze-frames and lurid montages, this script was immediately rejected by Friedkin whom Blatty had personally selected as the only man capable of bringing his novel to the screen. An Oscar-winning director, and an extremely accomplished script editor, Friedkin objected to the narrative complexity of Blatty's first-draft screenplay, and stingingly informed the author that he wouldn't use it because it was 'unfaithful to the novel'. Rather than working on a series of ad hoc revisions, Friedkin simply insisted that they start again from scratch, and presented Blatty with a marked-up copy of his own novel with scenes for inclusion in the film clearly delineated by the director. It was from this that Blatty fashioned the revised shooting script of *The Exorcist*, which is published here for the first time, offering a fascinating insight into the movie that Blatty and Friedkin set out to make when filming began on 14 August 1972.

Missing the distracting subplots which Blatty had initially transposed wholesale from his novel, this revised screenplay nevertheless included key scenes which the author felt were crucial to understanding the message of *The Exorcist*. During the lengthy filming process, further changes were made to this screenplay by

Blatty at Friedkin's request, sometimes to increase the verbal obscenities of the demon's attacks from which Blatty had initially shied, elsewhere to tone down any clear explanations of the events depicted, which the director always insisted the audience should interpret for themselves.

But while those alterations made during shooting were jointly agreed upon by the writer and director, other more significant changes happened during the editing of *The Exorcist* when Friedkin autonomously sliced scenes whose omission Blatty sorely mourned. These included an early scene of Regan (Linda Blair) exhibiting a melancholy preoccupation with death during a birthday outing; a conversation between Chris (Ellen Burstyn) and Doctor Klein (Barton Heyman) which built up a more gradual onset of Regan's disorder and set the scene for her later use of verbal obscenities; and a sentimental, upbeat epilogue in which Father Dyer (Father William O'Malley) and Lieutenant Kinderman (Lee J. Cobb) strike up an unlikely friendship by the site of Father Karras' final sacrificial fall.

Most significantly, Friedkin also snipped an exchange between Father Merrin (Max von Sydow) and Father Karras (Jason Miller) during a lull in the exorcism in which the ageing priest explicitly verbalizes the *reason* for Regan's possession – that the demon's target is not the little girl, but 'us', the observers, for whom Regan's suffering is intended as a cause for despair. As Friedkin has subsequently said; 'To me, the whole movie is about what they're talking about so *why are they talking about it?*' Blatty disagreed, but his protestations were in vain. By the time *The Exorcist* opened on Boxing Day 1973, it was about fifteen minutes shorter than the director's first fine cut which Blatty had enthusiastically endorsed, but which Friedkin subsequently opted to streamline into a two-hour roller-coaster ride.

Despite (or possibly *because of*) the cuts which Friedkin imposed, *The Exorcist* became one the biggest-grossing movies of its day, garnering ten Academy Award nominations, dividing critics and audiences who seemed in equal measure elated and appalled by the movie, and sparking an international wave of interest in the subject of demonic possession and the mysteries of the supernatural.

Mark Kermode, 1998

William Peter Blatty (right) with William Friedkin during the shoot of *The Exorcist*.

FADE IN:

Warner logo followed by minimal opening titles done in black lettering on white background. We then lose the final title, retaining the white background which quickly gives way to:

Full shot. Broiling noon sun.

EXT. EXCAVATION SITE. NINEVEH. DAWN

An Old Man in khakis works at section of mound with excavating pick. (In background there may be two Kurdish Assistants carefully packing the day's finds.) The Old Man now makes a find. He extracts it gingerly from the mound, begins to dust it off, then reacts with dismay upon recognizing a green stone amulet in the figure of the demon Pazuzu.

Close shot. Perspiration pouring down Old Man's brow.

Close shot. Old Man's hands. Trembling, they reach across a rude wooden table and cup themselves around a steaming glass of hot tea, as if for warmth.

Close shot. Old Man's face. The eyes staring off, haunted, as if by some chilling premonition – and some frightening remembrance.

EXT. LONG SHOT. ROADSIDE. CHAYKHANA. ERBIL AREA. DAY

SUPERIMPOSE: NORTHERN IRAQ

The chaykhana (teahouse) is set among poppied, green hills and athwart a ragged, rock-strewn bolt of road. In the background, the beautiful mound city of Erbil floats upward, scraping the clouds. The Kurdish Proprietor is seen leaning in the chaykhana doorway. He watches the only other character visible, the Old Man, who sits at an outdoor table, inexplicably cold beneath the fiery sun. Abstractedly, he sips at his tea. Nearby, parked off the road, an ancient jeep. LOSE SUPER. *The Proprietor shuffles out, stands beside the Old Man, speaks to him in Kurdish indistinctly. The Old Man appears not to hear at*

3

first, then comes to, looks up at Kurd, shakes head mutely, and reaches into the shirt pocket, removing coins to pay for his tea.

Close shot. Coins slipped on to table.

Close shot. Ignition key in jeep. The Old Man's hand reaches into frame, starts engine. The jeep takes off, disappearing down the road. The Kurd comes into frame, and we end CLOSE *on him as he watches the jeep. Mirrored in his face are sadness, love, respect.*

INT. ROOM IN MOSUL. CURATOR OF ANTIQUITIES' OFFICE. DAY

The camera is in motion, slowly panning the tagged finds of a recent archeological dig now spread out in neat rows on a long table. The camera stops finally at an Assyrian pendant as the Curator's hand reaches into frame, lifting the tag on the pendant so that the writing on it can be read by him. The only sound is the soft, regular ticking of an old-fashioned pendulum clock.

Close shot. Ledger containing entries of the finds. It is clearly headed (in the Curator's handwriting) 'Nineveh Excavation: Merrin'. On a fresh line of the entries, the Curator's hand now writes: 'Pendant, Assyrian; Palace of Assurbani –' Here, the hand breaks off.

Close shot. Arab Curator. He is seated at same table on which rest the finds and is looking up curiously from ledger at someone off-screen.

Close shot. Old Man. He is standing over another section of the same table. He is staring down at something on it off-screen.

Close shot. Amulet on table. Tagged – it is the Pazuzu amulet.

Close shot. Curator. His gaze is now on the amulet.

CURATOR
(*softly*)

Evil against evil.

Intercut. Old Man and Curator. The Old Man does not react, continuing to stare down at amulet, his expression haunted. After a beat:

Father?

We are on the Old Man now as, after several beats, the ticking of the

4

clock abruptly ceases; and it is this sudden silence that, after a beat, unconsciously causes the Old Man to look up at the Curator, who is still staring at him. Still no response. Something is worrying the Curator, but he doesn't know what.

CURATOR
(in Arabic)

My heart has a wish: that you would not go, old friend.

OLD MAN
(in Arabic)

I have an errand.

On Curator and Old Man. They stand by an open door to the street; the Old Man is about to leave. The Curator has hold of the Old Man's hand in both of his. He is troubled, as if the Old Man's premonition has invaded him. The Old Man slowly looks up at the Curator, searching his face with great affection. Then, with a squeeze of his hand:

Goodbye.

EXT. CURATOR'S OFFICE. DAY

The Old Man exits, leaving frame as he steps into the gathering gloom of the streets of Mosul. The Curator watches him, great love in his expression as:

POV: The Old Man. Street outside Curator's office. The Old Man almost collides with a fast-moving droshky.

Close moving shot. Droshky's sole passenger. A corpulent, Old Arab Woman in black, her face a shadow behind the lace veil draped loosely over her like a shroud.

On Curator. His expression darkening at this.

EXT. LONG SHOT. MOSUL OUTSKIRTS. NINEVEH EXCAVATION. DUSK

The Old Man is slowly and warily walking amid the ruins of a former temple area.

Old Man's POV: An Arab Watchman approaches, rifle at the ready, but then stops and waves as he recognizes the Old Man.

Moving shot as the Old Man slowly resumes his walk with the manner of someone sifting vibrations. He is like one looking for something, yet is afraid that he will find it. At last, upon seeing something off-screen, he freezes.

POV: Full shot: statue of Demon Pazuzu in situ. On Old Man. This is it. He lowers head, closing eyes against a dread confirmation of his premonition. A shadow of the statue lengthens and creeps on to the Old Man's face as, in the distance, we hear the dim yappings of savage dog packs.

Angle on shadows quickening across the desert. Still the dogs, yelping and howling distantly. A breeze rises up, blowing dust and sand across the frame.

On Old Man. He slowly lifts his head, his gaze on the off-screen statue of Pazuzu. But in his expression now is acceptance and grim determination. The shadow on his face has grown longer and the breeze is whipping gently at his shirt.

Old Man's POV: statue of Pazuzu.

6

High down shot. Temple area. Statue. Old Man.

They stand motionless like two ancient enemies squared off in a massive arena.

Angle on setting sun. It sinks into darkness. The dog packs.

EXT. SUNRISE SHOT. WASHINGTON, DC.

The sound of savage dogs gives way to distant sounds of friendly neighborhood dogs, children's voices, a city waking up.

SERIES OF MOVING SHOTS. GEORGETOWN AREA. DAWN

Below us, the Potomac River; the Gothic spires and wooded walks of Georgetown University; a Priest or two walking, saying their Office; and then we are on Prospect Street, slowly approaching a house that sits beside a flight of steep, stone steps plunging precipitately down to 'M' Street below. An upstairs bedroom light is burning.

INT. CHRIS MACNEIL'S BEDROOM. DAWN

Chris is sitting up in bed. Her lips move silently as she studies lines from a film script. We hear light, off-screen rapping sounds; irregular, yet rhythmically clustered, like alien code tapped out by a dead man. Chris hears them, listens for a moment, then tries to ignore them, but she cannot concentrate. She irritably slams the script down and flounces out of bed. She exits into:

INT. MACNEIL HOUSE. SECOND-FLOOR HALL. DAWN

The rappings are louder. Chris listens for the source of the sound, locates it, throws open the door to Regan's bedroom.

INT. REGAN'S BEDROOM. CHRIS AT DOOR. DAWN

The rappings have ceased abruptly. Chris looks baffled.

POV: The room. Camera shifting to follow Chris's scrutiny. It is a typical child's bedroom. A large bay window with shutters overlooks the steps outside the house. Regan is asleep, her blankets kicked off and askew. Chris moves to the bedside. Heavy breathing, regular and deep. Chris considers, then abruptly notices goose pimples on her arms. She

7

rubs at them, shivering as if at an icy coldness. She touches the nearby radiator. Hot. She looks at Regan, frowning in perplexity, for Regan's brow is wet with perspiration. Chris squints her eyes in consternation; looks back at her goose pimples. Now she hears sounds from above, like tiny claws scratching at the edge of a galaxy. She looks up at ceiling. The scrapings cease. Chris keeps staring a moment, then looks down. She leans over, adjusts Regan's pillow, then examines her features with warmth.

CHRIS
(whisper)

I sure do love you.

Car lights reflect on the ceiling of the darkened room.

INT. MACNEIL HOUSE. KITCHEN. CLOSE ON BACON FRYING. DAY

CHRIS
(off-screen)

Hi, Willie. Howya doin'?

Full shot. Kitchen. Chris and Willie.

Willie, a middle-aged housekeeper, is at the stove. Sleepy-eyed Chris, in bathrobe and carrying a script, is entering. Willie hastily puts down her fork, wiping hands on a dish towel as:

WILLIE
(German accent)

Oh, Mrs MacNeil! Good morning!

As Willie moves for the coffee pot, Chris is ahead of her.

CHRIS

Never mind, Willie, I'll get it.

She drops a pack of cigarettes and matches beside her cup and sits. Crusty-eyed, she picks up copy of the Washington Post *by plate and stares at it fuddled until she realizes it is upside down. She turns it right-side up. A man enters: Karl. Willie's husband. Very Teutonic. He is carrying a Sparklett's bottle to mount on cooler in exchange for the empty.*

8

KARL

Good morning, madam.

CHRIS
(*lights cigarette*)

Mornin'. Hey, Karl, we've got rats in the attic. Better get us some traps.

KARL

There are rats?

CHRIS

I just said that.

KARL

But the attic is clean.

CHRIS

Well, okay, we've got tidy rats.

KARL

No rats.

CHRIS

Karl, I heard them this *morning*!

KARL

Maybe plumbing. Maybe boards.

CHRIS

Maybe *rats*! Now will you buy the damn traps and quit arguing?

KARL
(*leaving quickly*)

Yes. I go now.

CHRIS

No, not *now*, Karl! The *stores* are all closed.

KARL

I will see.

CHRIS

Karl – !

Karl is gone. Chris and Willie exchange exasperated glances, and then we hear the front door open and close, off-screen. With a sigh, Willie turns back to the bacon, shaking her head.

WILLIE

They are closed.

EXT. CAMPUS OF GEORGETOWN UNIVERSITY. DAY

A film is being shot in front of the steps of Healy Building. The usual equipment, cast and crew are in evidence, as well as spectators made up of faculty and students. Chris, in jeans and sweatshirt, and indicating page in her script (titled 'Crash Course'), calls her director, elfin, British Burke Dennings. He has been drinking. Swigging from a paper cup, he looks over as:

CHRIS
(argumentatively)
Hey, Burke? Take a look at the damned thing, will ya?

DENNINGS

Oh, how marvelous! You *do* have a script, I see!
(surgically shaves a narrow strip from the edge of the page of her script)
Yes, how nice! I believe I'll just have a little munchie.

As they continue, Burke will nervously fiddle with the paper, then begin to chew on it. In the meantime:

CHRIS

Burke –

DENNINGS

Yes, I'm *terribly* glad that the star has a script. Now then, tell me, my baby: What is it? What's wrong?

CHRIS
(indicating script)
It just doesn't make sense.

DENNINGS
(lying)
Why, it's perfectly plain. You're a teacher at the college and you don't want the building torn down and –

CHRIS

Oh, well, Jesus, Burke. Thanks. I can read.

DENNINGS

Then what's wrong?

CHRIS

Why the hell should they tear down the building?

DENNINGS

Are you sending me up?

CHRIS

No, I'm asking 'What for?'

DENNINGS

Because it's *there*!

CHRIS

In the script?

DENNINGS

(suppressing drunken giggle)

On the *grounds*!

CHRIS

Well, it doesn't make sense. They wouldn't do that.

DENNINGS

They would!

CHRIS

No, they *wouldn't*!

DENNINGS

Shall we summon the writer? I believe he's in Paris!

CHRIS

Hiding?

DENNINGS

Fucking! Now then, shall we get on with it?

Chris stares momentarily, then sags on to Burke spurting laughter. Then she looks worriedly toward a priest (Damien Karras) off-screen among the spectators, afraid he's heard the obscenity. And now we cut to

*Karras and see that he is smiling slightly but warmly. The angle then
returns to Chris, Burke and the Assistant Director.*

I said, 'Shall we get *on* with it?'

CHRIS
Huh? Yeah, okay, Burke. Let's go.

DENNINGS
(*to Assistant Director*)
All right, lights, love.

ASSISTANT DIRECTOR
Let's warm 'em!

DENNINGS
(*to Assistant Director*)
Now the extras should be . . .

*And we hear the ad lib continuation off-screen a bit as the camera now
follows Chris as she walks, head down, concentrating while the crew sets
up. Then she looks over toward Karras. He's gone. She sees him
walking slowly away toward the campus gates like a lone black cloud in
search of the rain. Dennings comes to Chris.*

Are you ready, ducks?

CHRIS
Do it.

DENNINGS
Roll the film.

ASSISTANT DIRECTOR
Okay, roll 'em.

TECHNICIAN
Speed.

DENNINGS
Action!

*While Extras cheer and boo at her approach, Chris races up the Healy
steps and seizes bullhorn from a Rebel Student Leader. There is pushing
and shoving. Police are on the scene.*

CHRIS
(*through bullhorn*)
Okay, now, hold it! Hold it a second!
(*as the commotion continues*)
Hey, give me a chance, will ya, huh? Just a minute?

We see now that various of the student factions are holding up signs and banners. Some read: 'KEEP CLASSES OPEN', 'FREE LOGIC!', 'SHUT DOWN!', 'CLOSE THE SCHOOL' *and* 'BURN IT!?' *Still other placards are* blank. *Many of the Students in one sector are affecting shrouds and death masks. As the commotion diminishes:*

Look, we're all concerned with human rights, but the kids who pay tuition have also got a right, the right to learn, and shutting those kids out of class solves nothing. It's answering one kind of tyranny with another, one kind of cruelty with another.

Commotion. At some point during the above speech, we will hear Chris off-screen while the camera goes to Dennings as the director turns a significant and imperious gaze to the Assistant Director, who dutifully

pads over to him and proffers his open script like an aging altar boy
proffers the missal to his priest at solemn Mass. Burke begins to slice off
a fresh strip of page.

EXT. 'O' STREET. CAMPUS MAIN GATE. DAY

It has clouded over, threatening rain. Chris, wearing a raincoat, sends
the limo driver home.

CHRIS
I feel like walking, Tommy. Thanks.

Tommy nods. Chris starts to walk home, thoughtful and weary. As she
walks by Holy Trinity Auditorium, a Young Priest in nylon windbreaker
passes her. Tense. He takes a right into an easement leading into a
courtyard at the back of church. Chris pauses by the easement, watching
him; curious. He heads for a white frame cottage from which an Older
Priest emerges looking glum and nervous. He nods curtly toward the
Young Priest, and with lowered eyes heads for a door to the back of the
church. Again, the cottage door opens from within and Karras appears.
He silently greets the Young Priest, putting his arm around his shoulder as
he leads him inside, a gesture that is gentle and somehow parental. The
door closes and they are gone. Chris is pensive, puzzled by the scene. A
rumble of thunder. She looks up at the sky, tugging up raincoat collar.

EXT. MACNEIL HOUSE. DUSK

Chris enters.

INT. MACNEIL HOUSE. KITCHEN. DUSK

We open on Sharon Spencer, a pretty young blonde and Chris's
secretary (and nurse to Regan) sitting at the breakfast table, typing.
Stack of mail and messages. We hear the front door close; footsteps
approaching. Chris enters, weary.

SHARON
(*continuing to type*)
Hi, Chris. How'd it go?

CHRIS
Oh, well, it was kind of like the Walt Disney version of the Ho
Chi Minh story, but other than that it was really terrific.

14

Chris has come to the table, stands leafing through mail and messages.
Sharon continues to type through:

Anything exciting?

SHARON

Do you want to have dinner next week at the White House?

CHRIS

Are you kidding?

SHARON

No, of course not; it's Thursday.

CHRIS

Big party?

SHARON

No, I gather it's just five or six people.

CHRIS
(back to the table sifting mail and messages)
No kidding? Where's Rags?

SHARON

Oh, she's down in the playroom.

CHRIS

What doin'?

SHARON

She's sculpting. She's making you a bird.

CHRIS

How'd the lesson go?

SHARON
(frowning)
Bad time with math again.

CHRIS

Oh? Gee, that's funny.

SHARON

I know. It's her favorite subject.

CHRIS

Oh, well, this 'new math'. Christ, I couldn't make change for
the bus if –

*She is interrupted by the bounding entrance of Regan, her eleven-year-
old daughter. Freckles. Ponytails. Braces on teeth. Arms outstretched,
she is racing for her mother.*

REGAN

Hi, Mom!

*She is in the scene now as Chris catches her in a bear-hug. Sharon
resumes her typing.*

CHRIS

Hiya, bearface!

*Chris covers Regan with smacking kisses. Then, rocking her back and
forth:*

What'd ya do today? Anything exciting?

REGAN

Oh, stuff.

CHRIS

So, what *kind* of stuff?

REGAN

Oh, well, I studied, and I painted.

CHRIS

Wha'd ya paint?

REGAN

Oh, well, flowers. Ya know, daisies? An' – Oh! Mother! This
horse!
                    (excited; eyes widening)
This man had a horse, ya know, down by the river? We were
talking, see, Mom, and then along came this *horse*! He was
beautiful! Oh, Mom, ya should've *seen* him, and the man let
me *sit* on him! *Really*! I mean, practically a *minute*! It was a
gray horse! Mother, can't we get a horse? I mean, *could* we?

CHRIS

We'll see, baby.

REGAN

Gee, Mom, I'm starving.

CHRIS

Run upstairs and get dressed and we'll go out for some pizza.

Regan races upstairs.

REGAN

Can I wear my new dress?

CHRIS

Honey, sure.
                    (*to Sharon*)
Got a date?

SHARON

Yes, I do.

CHRIS

You go on, then.
                    (*indicating mail*)
We can catch all this stuff in the morning.

Sharon rises, but Chris abruptly recollects something.

Oh, hey, wait. There's a letter got to go out tonight.

SHARON
(*reaching for dictation pad*)

Oh, okay.

Chris starts to dictate:

CHRIS

Dear Mr Gable . . .

Sharon reacts, amused; then Chris dictates in earnest: a letter to her agent. As she gets into it:

REGAN
(*off-screen*)

Moth-theeeeeerrrr! I can't find the dress.

CHRIS

Guess I'd better go find it for her.

SHARON
(*eyeing watch*)
Gee, it's time for me to meditate, Chris.

CHRIS

You really think that kind of stuff is going to do you any good?

SHARON

Well, it gives me peace of mind.

CHRIS
(*after a long beat*)

Right.

She turns away and starts to exit.

Correct. Terrific.

INT. MACNEIL HOUSE. SECOND-FLOOR HALLWAY. DUSK

Chris heads for Regan's bedroom and enters.

INT. REGAN'S BEDROOM. DUSK

The scene is odd: Regan is standing in the middle of the room, silently staring up at the ceiling, frowning.

CHRIS

What's doin'?

REGAN

Funny noises.

CHRIS
(*moving to the clothes closet and searching for dress*)
I know. We've got friends.

REGAN

Huh?

Squirrels, honey. Squirrels in the attic.

Regan looks unconvinced. She looks up at the ceiling again; then moves over to watch her mother's search for the dress which now ends in apparent failure.

See, Mom? It's not there.

Yeah, I see. Maybe Willie picked it up with the cleaning.

It's gone.

(taking a dress off the rack)
Yeah, well, put on the navy. It's pretty.

EXT. 'C & O' CANAL. DUSK

Karras and the Georgetown University President (Tom) are walking.

KARRAS

It's my mother. She's alone, Tom. I never should've left her.
At least in New York I'd be close. I could see her.

TOM

I could see about a transfer.

KARRAS

I need reassignment. Get me out of this job, Tom; it's wrong.
It's no good.

TOM

Are you kidding? You're the best that we've got.

They stop.

KARRAS

Am I really? It's more than psychiatry, Tom, and you know
that. Some of their problems come down to vocation, to the
meaning of their lives, and I just can't cut it, Tom. It's too
much. I need out. I'm unfit.

After a pause.

I think I've lost my faith.

INT. BASEMENT PLAYROOM OF MACNEIL HOUSE. EARLY EVENING

Chris is coming down, calling to Regan.

CHRIS

Whatchya doin' down there?

REGAN

Come on down, Mom; I've got a surprise.

CHRIS

Oh, great.

*Regan is standing by a games table in the basement-made-over-as-
playroom, and hands her a sculpted clay 'worry bird' with a comically
long painted nose. Chris oohs and ahhs.*

REGAN

Do you like it?

CHRIS

Oh, honey, I do, I really do. Got a name for it?

REGAN

Uh-uh.

CHRIS

What's a good one?

REGAN
(*shrugging*)

I dunno.

CHRIS
(*pondering*)

Let me see, let me see. I don't know. Whaddya think?
Whaddya think about 'Dumbbird'? Huh? Just 'Dumbbird'.

Regan is snickering, nodding; hand to mouth to hide the braces.

'Dumbbird' by a landslide! Super!
(*setting bird on table*)
Here, I'll leave it here to dry for a . . .

She has noticed an Ouija board and planchette on the table.

Hey, where'd you get the Ouija board?

REGAN
(*indicating*)

I found it.

CHRIS

Found it where?

REGAN
(*indicating*)

In that closet.

CHRIS

You been playin' with it?

REGAN

Yep.

CHRIS
(*surprised*)

You know how?

REGAN
(*moving to sit by board*)
Oh, well, sure. Here, I'll show you.

CHRIS
Well, I think you need *two* people, honey.

REGAN
No, ya don't, Mom. I do it all the time.

CHRIS
(*pulling up chair opposite*)
Oh, you do? Well, let's both play, Okay?

REGAN

Well – okay.

Regan has her fingertips positioned on the planchette, and as Chris reaches out to put hers there, the planchette makes a sudden, forceful move to the 'No' position on the board.

CHRIS
You don't want me to play?

REGAN
No, I *do*! Captain *Howdy* said 'No'.

CHRIS

Captain who?

REGAN

Captain Howdy.

CHRIS
Honey, who's Captain Howdy?

REGAN
Oh, ya know. I make questions and he does the answers.

CHRIS

That so?

REGAN

Oh, he's nice.

CHRIS

Oh, well, sure; he's terrific.

REGAN

Here, I'll show you.

Regan stares at the board, eyes drawn tight in concentration.

Captain Howdy, do you think my mom is pretty?

Seconds tick by. Nothing happening. Chris turns her head at an odd, off-screen creaking sound from the closet area. She holds the look for a moment, then looks back at the board. Another few beats of silence. Then:

Captain Howdy?

(*no response*)

Captain Howdy, that's *really* not very *polite.*

CHRIS

Honey, maybe he's sleeping.

REGAN
(*muttering*)

Let him sleep on his *own* time.

INT. REGAN'S BEDROOM. NIGHT

Regan in bed. Chris finishing tucking her in. Sits on bed.

CHRIS

Honey, Sunday's your birthday. Want to do somethin'?

REGAN

What?

CHRIS

Oh, well, *I* don't know. Somethin'. You want to go see the sights?

REGAN

Oh, *yeah,* Mom!

23

CHRIS

And tomorrow night a movie! How's that?

REGAN
(*a hug*)

Oh, I love you!

CHRIS

Oh, Rags, honey, I love you.

REGAN

You can bring Mr Dennings if you like.

CHRIS

Mr Dennings?

REGAN

Well, I mean, it's okay.

CHRIS
(*chuckling*)

No, it isn't okay. Honey, why would I want to bring Burke?

REGAN

Well, you like him.

CHRIS

Oh, well, sure I like him, honey. Don't you?
(*no response*)
Baby, what's going on?

REGAN
(*a sullen statement*)

You're going to marry him, Mommy, aren't you?

CHRIS
(*amused*)

Oh, my baby, of *course* not! What on earth are you *talking* about? Burke Dennings? Where'd you get that idea?

REGAN

But you like him.

CHRIS

I like pizzas but I wouldn't ever marry one! Honey, he's a
friend, just a crazy old friend!

REGAN

You don't like him like Daddy?

CHRIS

Rags, I *love* your daddy. I'll *always* love your daddy. Mr
Dennings comes by here a lot 'cause he's lonely, that's all,
he's a friend.

REGAN

Well, I heard . . .

CHRIS

You heard what? Heard from who?

REGAN

I don't know. I just thought . . .

CHRIS

Well, it's silly, so forget it.

REGAN

Okay.

INT. MACNEIL HOUSE. STUDY. NIGHT

*Stretched out on rug in front of the fire, Chris studying the script. Turns
a page. Regan, half asleep, enters.*

CHRIS

Hi, honey. What's wrong?

REGAN

There's these real funny noises, Mom. It's like knocking. I
can't go to sleep.

CHRIS
(*struggling up*)
Oh, where the heck are those traps!

REGAN

Huh?

25

Chris takes her hand, leading her out of study.

CHRIS

Oh, nothing, hon. Come on. You can sleep in my bedroom
and I'll see what it is.

INT. CHRIS'S BEDROOM. NIGHT

Chris is tucking Regan into her (Chris's) bed.

REGAN

Can I watch TV for a while till I sleep?

CHRIS

Where's your book?

REGAN

I can't find it. Can I watch?

CHRIS
(turning on bedside TV)

Sure, okay.

(tunes volume control)

Loud enough?

REGAN

Yes.

CHRIS
(exiting; turning out light)

Try to sleep.

EXT. MACNEIL HOUSE. NIGHT

Full shot: In an upper floor gabled window we see candlelight glow.

INT. MACNEIL HOUSE. NIGHT

Down shot: On Chris as she climbs narrow steps to attic with candle.

INT. ATTIC. AT DOOR. NIGHT

*Door is pushed slowly open. Chris enters, tries the light switch. It doesn't
work. She looks about the attic searching for something while slowly*

26

advancing at the camera when the candle flame suddenly and astoundingly disengages from the candle and shoots up to the ceiling and is extinguished. Behind Chris, having come upstairs, looms Karl. Coming up silently behind Chris:

KARL

There is nothing.

On the 'Nothing', Chris leaps three feet out of her skin and emits a yelp of fright, spinning around and practically into Karl's arms. A hand to her fluttering heart:

CHRIS

Oh, good Jesus! Oh, Jesus H. *Christ*, Karl, don't *do* that!

KARL

Very sorry. But you see? No rats.

CHRIS

Yeah, no rats. Thanks a lot, Karl. Terrific.

> KARL
> (exiting)

Madam, maybe cat better.

> CHRIS

What?

> KARL

Maybe cat better – to catch rats.

He exits. Chris stares a moment, then releases a sigh of weariness and relief.

EXT. MACNEIL HOUSE. NIGHT

Bedroom light is turned off. All is peaceful.

EXT. MONTAGE. CHRIS AND REGAN SIGHTSEEING IN DC. MEMORIAL DRIVE AND LEE MANSION. DAY

Giving way to:

Chris and Regan at Tomb of Unknown Soldier.

They stare mutely. Regan has turned sad. After a few beats:

> REGAN
>
> Mom, why do people have to die?

Chris looks at her. She doesn't know how to answer. Finally:

> CHRIS
> *(tenderly)*
>
> Honey, people get tired.

> REGAN
>
> Why does God let them?

> CHRIS
> *(frowning, a few beats)*
>
> Who's been telling you about God, baby?

> REGAN
>
> Sharon.

> CHRIS
>
> Oh.

> REGAN
>
> Mom, why does God *let* us get tired?

> CHRIS
> *(after a beat)*
>
> Well, after a while, God gets lonesome for us, Rags. He wants
> us back.

INT. CHRIS MACNEIL'S BEDROOM. NIGHT

*Chris is pacing with the phone receiver to her ear, waiting, and in the
meantime is talking to Sharon, who is seated on the edge of the bed,
scribbling shorthand in a steno pad.*

> CHRIS
>
> And get hold of that real estate agent and tell him we're
> staying till June. I want Rags to finish up the semester at
> school. And then –
> *(half talk into phone)*
> Yeah, yeah, I'm here. Yes, I'm waiting . . .

> (*mouthpiece down, to Sharon*)
> Good Christ, do you believe it?

INT. MACNEIL HOUSE. SECOND-FLOOR HALL. NIGHT

Despondent, Regan stands head down, hand on doorknob to her bedroom, listening to:

> CHRIS
> (*off-screen*)
> Doesn't send a card or call his daughter on her birthday?

> SHARON
> (*off-screen*)
> Well, the circuits might be busy.

> CHRIS
> (*off-screen*)
> My ass, he just doesn't *give* a shit! He's just –

Regan sadly enters her room as:

> (*off-screen; phone*)
> *Yes*, goddammit, I'm *waiting*!

INT. CHRIS'S BEDROOM. NIGHT

> CHRIS
> (*pacing; muttering to herself*)
> The whole fucking world is still waiting for the sunrise.

INT. CHRIS'S BEDROOM. DAWN

We are on Chris in bed as the phone rings. She answers. Wake-up call from the Assistant Director. Hangs up; gets out of bed; discovers Regan is in bed with her, half awake.

> CHRIS
> Well, what in the – !
> (*amused*)
> What are you doing *here?*

REGAN

My bed was shaking.

CHRIS

Oh, you nut.
(kisses her and pulls up her covers)
Go back to sleep.

EXT. HOUSE. NIGHT TO DAY TRANSITION

Follow Newspaper Boy on bike to Holy Trinity.

INT. HOLY TRINITY CHURCH AT REAR SIDE DOOR. DAWN

We hear key in door from the other side. The Pastor of Holy Trinity sluggishly enters, sets door stop to hold the door open, turns on the church lights, blows his nose into a handkerchief as he absently shuffles along; then genuflects at the altar railing. He says a silent prayer, and as he looks up and starts to bless himself he reacts with startlement and then shock as he sees before him:

POV: Statue of Blessed Virgin at side altar. It has been desecrated, painted over to suggest that the Virgin is a harlot. A slatternly, dissolute appearance. And glued to the appropriate spot is a sculpted clay phallus in erection.

INT. NEW YORK SUBWAY STATION. DAY

Silence, except for the low rumble of a distant train. Points of light stretch down the darkness of the tunnel like guides to hopelessness.

Angle on platform. Man. The station appears to be deserted. The Man stands close to the edge of the near platform. Black coat, hat and trousers. Powerfully built. He carries a valise resembling a doctor's medical bag, and stands with his back to us, head down, as if in dejection. Near him, a vending machine on a pillar.

Wide angle. Platform.

DERELICT

Faddah.

An old Derelict lies drunk, his back against the station wall.

Hey, Faddah! Couldja help an old altar boy, Faddah? I'm Cat'lic.

The Man looks up with dismay, disclosing the round Roman collar at the neck, and the face of Damien Karras, now filled with an even deeper pain than when we met him before. He shuts his eyes against this intrusion and clutches at his coat lapels, pulling them together as if to hide the collar. The train sound is up full now, and in another angle the train rushes across frame, blocking our view of Karras and the Derelict.

EXT. EAST 21ST STREET IN NEW YORK. DAY

High shot: Between 1st and 2nd Avenues. Karras walks despondently along the south side of the street, which is studded with decrepit tenement buildings. He pauses before one and with melancholy sees his past in the raggedly clothed, grim-covered, foul-mouthed urchins pitching pennies against the stoop. Karras looks up at front door. He starts up the steps.

INT. KARRAS'S MOTHER'S APARTMENT BUILDING. HALL. DAY

Karras. Cutting, we find the camera stationed by an apartment front door, trained on Karras mounting steps at the far end of the hall. He approaches and lightly raps. From within we hear faint sound of a radio tuned to a news station. Karras waits a moment, then digs out a key from his pants pocket, opens the door like an aching wound, and enters.

INT. TENEMENT APARTMENT. DAY

The radio is now more audible. We are in a railroad-flat kitchen. Tiny. Cracking plaster and peeling wallpaper. Unkempt. Sparse and ancient furnishings. In the kitchen, a small tub for bathing. Faded old newspapers spread on the uncarpeted floor. As Karras enters, he breathes in an aching sigh as his gaze brushes around at the painful reminders of his past. Then he glances to the right, from which we hear the sound of the radio. He puts down the valise and starts into the bedroom.

KARRAS

Mama?

No response. The camera follows him into a squalid living-room. Karras now sees his Mother, fully dressed, sleeping on a torn and grease-stained old sofa. On her right cheek, a prominent mole. He observes her for a moment, sighs as he removes his raincoat.

As he drapes it over a chair, his Mother awakens with a slight start, sees him, reacts with surprise and joy. Speaking with a thick Mediterranean accent:

MOTHER

Dimmy!

She hastily gets to her feet and throws her arms around Karras.

Oh, Dimmy, I so glad to see you!

INT. KARRAS'S MOTHER'S KITCHEN. DAY

We hear the radio still tuned to news. Karras and Mother sit at a tiny table in the kitchen. Karras sips at his coffee. His Mother drinks in his presence as:

33

MOTHER

Dimmy, you thin. You not eating.
(*rising*)

I fix for you.

KARRAS

No, Mom.

MOTHER

I fix.

CUT TO:

Karras and Mother at the table. Karras eating.

KARRAS

Really great, Mom! Just great!

MOTHER

You Uncle John come by to visit me.

KARRAS
(*pleased*)

Oh really, Ma? When?

MOTHER

Last month.

Karras looks saddened.

INT. MOTHER'S LIVING-ROOM. NIGHT

Mother (wearing holy medal) sits on the sofa, watching as Karras repairs a broken lamp. The room has been tidied up a little. In the scene we see a broom, a small plastic refuse container and a dilapidated carpet sweeper. Silence. Then:

MOTHER

Dimmy, you worry about something?

KARRAS

No, Mama.

MOTHER

You not happy. What's the matter, Dimmy?

34

KARRAS

Nothing, Mama. Really. I'm fine.

A pause. Then:

MOTHER
(*off-screen*)

I wish you was marry Mary McArdle.

Close shot. Mother silently watching; thinking.

Another angle. (Time passage.) Karras is entering the living-room, pulling on his raincoat. He has his valise. He comes to Mother and observes her sadly for a moment. Regret. He leans over and kisses her cheek tenderly. He starts to leave, remembers something, tunes the radio to all-news station.

EXT. FORDHAM UNIVERSITY. DAWN

Establishing shot.

INT. JESUIT RESIDENCE HALL. SMALL CHAPEL. DAWN

Karras wears trousers and a T-shirt. He vests and prepares for Mass, and then steps back facing the altar, blesses himself, and begins:

KARRAS
(*with poignant longing*)

'I will go to the Altar of God,
Unto God who gives joy to my youth.'

INT. HALL OF BELLEVUE HOSPITAL. DAY

The camera is fixed at one end of the hall, and Karras and his Uncle are approaching from far down the opposite end; however, their dialogue is clearly audible at all times, and their voices metallically reverberant. Karras has his head down, sorrowful and dismayed, as he listens to the Uncle, who speaks with a thick, immigrant accent. Karras is ruefully shaking his head, and the Uncle is gesturing helplessly, defensively, as:

UNCLE

But, Dimmy, da edema affected her *brain*! You understand? She don't let any doctor come *near* her! She was all da time screamin', even talkin' to da radio! Listen, regular hospital

35

not gonna put *up* wit' dat, Dimmy! Un'erstan'? So we give
her a shot an' bring her here 'til da doctors, day fix up her leg!
Den we take her right out, Dimmy. Two or t'ree month, and
she's out, good as new.

*Another angle. Karras and his Uncle have halted outside a locked door
above which is posted the legend: Neuro-Psychiatric: Ward 3, and
Uncle pushes buzzer to summon Nurse.*

You go in, Dimmy. I wait out here.

Karras nods. Now the Uncle has his head down in ironic thought.

Dat's funny. You know, if you wasn't be priest, you be
famous psychiatrist now on Park Avenue, Dimmy. Your
mother, she be livin' in a penthouse instead of da –

INT. WARD 3 AT PADDED ENTRY DOOR. DAY

*As a corpulent Nurse waddles into frame and uses a large iron key to
unlock door, off-screen, we hear the demented screams, moans and
fragmented statements of mental patients. The door comes open, disclosing
Karras and Uncle. Karras slowly lifts his head at the off-screen sounds.*

INT. WARD 3. INVALIDED PATIENTS' ROOM. DAY

*Karras walks down the aisle of an enormous ward containing eighty
beds. The Patients are mostly elderly, and we hear their cries of pain
and demented chatter. Karras stops before a bedded patient far down the
row: his Mother. Gaunt and hollow-eyed, looking confused and helpless;
disoriented; she has spied her son and is gripping at the sidebars of
the bed, trying to raise herself as the camera now moves forward again,
trained on Mother. By the time Karras halts by her, Mother, looking
frightened and pathetic, eyes wide with pleading, has raised herself up,
pulling weakly, hands trembling.*

MOTHER
Why you do dis to me, Dimmy? Why?

INT. BELLEVUE HALL. DAY

*Karras and Uncle walking. Behind them, Ward 3 entry door. Karras is
fumbling for his cigarette pack. His eyes are wet with tears.*

KARRAS

Couldn't you have put her someplace else?

UNCLE

Like what? Private hospital? Who got da money for dat, Dimmy? You?

INT. GYM. DAY

Karras in boxer shorts and shirt works savagely at a punching bag of the man-sized, stuffed variety. Eyes wet with tears, he slams at the bag with a mixture of sorrow, rage and frustration.

INT. DR KLEIN'S OFFICE. ROSSLYN BUILDING. DAY

Chris sits in the reception room. A few other Mothers and Children are present.

INT. DR KLEIN'S EXAMINING-ROOM. DAY

Brief montage of shots.

Klein administering a physical to Regan. Should include ophthalmoscope, tuning fork and simple coordination test. Also blood sample in centrifograph, and urine sample under microscope. Final shot has a Nurse leaning with her back against the examining table, her expression partly puzzled, partly disturbed as she observes Regan, who is in her slip and in constant motion; stepping, twirling, touching, making nervous movements while aimlessly humming. Klein is not present.

INT. DR KLEIN'S OFFICE. DAY

Chris is seated on the edge of a chair. Klein is behind his desk, writing a prescription.

KLEIN

A disorder of the nerves. At least we think it is. We don't know yet exactly how it works, but it's often seen in early adolescence. She shows all the symptoms: the hyperactivity; the temper; her performance in math.

CHRIS

Yeah, the math. Why the math?

37

KLEIN

It affects concentration.
(*rips the prescription from the small blue pad and hands it over*)
Now this is for Ritalin. Ten milligrams a day.

CHRIS
(*eyes prescription*)
What is it? A tranquilizer?

KLEIN

A stimulant.

CHRIS
*Stim*ulant? She's higher'n a kite right *now*!

KLEIN

Her condition isn't quite what it seems. Nobody knows the cause of hyperkinetic behaviour in a child. The Ritalin seems to work to relieve the condition, but we really don't know how or why, frankly. Your daughter's symptoms could be an overreaction to depression – but that's out of my field.

CHRIS

Depression?

KLEIN
Well, you mentioned her father . . . the divorce.

CHRIS
Do you think I should take her to see a psychiatrist?

KLEIN
Oh, no. I'd wait and see what happens with the Ritalin. I think that's the answer. Wait two or three weeks.

CHRIS
And those lies she's been telling?

KLEIN

Lies?

CHRIS
Ya know, those things to get attention, like saying that her bed shakes and stuff.

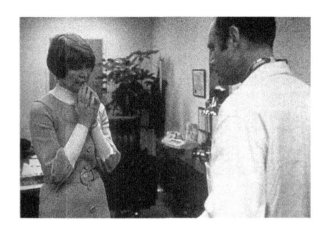

KLEIN

Have you ever known your daughter to swear and use
obscenities?

CHRIS

Never.

KLEIN

Well, you see, that's quite similar to things like her lying –
uncharacter –

CHRIS
(interrupting, perplexed)
Wait a minute. What are you talking about?

KLEIN

Well, she let loose quite a string while I was examining her,
Mrs MacNeil.

CHRIS

You're kidding! Like what?

KLEIN

(*looking evasive*)

Well, I'd say her vocabulary's rather extensive.

CHRIS

Well, what, for example? I mean, give me a for instance!

Klein shrugs. No reply.

Hey, come on; I'm grown-up. What'd she *say*? I mean
specifically, Doctor.

KLEIN

Well, specifically, Mrs MacNeil, she advised me to keep my
fingers away from her 'goddam cunt'.

CHRIS

(*shocked*)

She used those words?

KLEIN

She used those words. Look, I doubt that she even
understood what she was saying.

CHRIS

Yeah, I guess. Maybe not. You don't think a psychiatrist – ?

KLEIN

The best explanation is always the simplest one. Let's wait.
Let's wait and see.

(*smiling encouragingly*)

In the meantime, try not to worry.

CHRIS

How?

INT. MACNEIL HOME. LIVING-ROOM. NIGHT

*Full shot: party in progress. A few Jesuits and some of the cast and crew
of the motion picture are present. Vibrant hum of conversation. Then a
closer angle featuring Burke Dennings. Burke, an empty glass in hand,
stands chatting with a silver-maned Senator and the Senator's Wife.
Back of them, and to the side, Chris is visible, chatting with the Jesuit*

Dean of the college. Karl is approaching the latter with a drinks tray.
Burke seems irritable and tautly drunk.

DENNINGS

No, no, *her* part is finished; all the parts with the principal
actors, you see; but I'm staying to finish other scenes.

SENATOR

I understand.

Karl has searched Burke's group.

DENNINGS

Oh, how splendid.
(reaching for a fresh drink)
Let's have another for the road.

CHRIS
(brief over-the-shoulder at Dennings)
The Lincoln Highway?

DENNINGS
(to Chris)
Oh, now, don't be so silly.

SENATOR'S WIFE
(to Chris)
Fun party.

CHRIS
(to wife)
Thanks, Martha.

And Chris returns to conversation with the Dean. During the above, the
Senator has mutely refused another drink, but Burke now takes one in
his other *hand as well as:*

DENNINGS
(to Karl)
Karl, oh, now tell me, was it *Public* Relations you did for the
Gestapo, or *Community* Relations? I believe there's a
difference.

KARL
(*grimly uptight*)

I am Swiss.

DENNINGS
Yes, of course. And you never went bowling with Goebbels, I
suppose.

*Front tracking shot. Karl, his face impassive; yet his eyes are angry, as
we hear:*

(*to Karl as latter moves on*)
So superior, aren't you? Nazi!

*The camera follows Karl but holds – as he passes them – on Sharon and
Mary Jo Perrin, who are seated somewhere in the room. A bubbly
personality, Mary Jo is reading Sharon's palm.*

PERRIN
Well, yes, your work line is longer than your heart line.
There, you see? And you've recently broken up with a
boyfriend. Am I right?

SHARON

No.

PERRIN
I'm really famous for predictions, not palms.
(*dropping Sharon's palm*)
Where's the bathroom?

SHARON
(*rising*)
Upstairs. I'll go with you.

As they move, the camera follows:

PERRIN
Oh, by the way, I brought that witchcraft book you asked for.

SHARON
Oh, thanks.

PERRIN
And another one on Russian ESP. They're in the study.

They walk out of frame as the camera holds on Dennings, the Senator and his Wife. The Senator is turned away from Dennings, conversing in low tones with Wife. Dennings is now composed and as he stares down into his gin glass:

DENNINGS

There seems to be an alien pubic hair in my gin.

SENATOR
(turning to Dennings, as his Wife splits)
I beg your pardon?

DENNINGS
(defensive)
Never seen it before in my *life*!

SENATOR
(a murmur)

Yes, I'm sure.

DENNINGS
(now accusatory)

Have you?

Angle on Chris, Jesuit Dean, Mary Jo Perrin. Mary Jo is seated on the sofa with Jesuit Dean. Chris is on the floor in front of the coffee table facing them, as all eat dinner.

PERRIN

On, come on, every family's got one black sheep.

DEAN

Yes, I know, but we were pushing our quota with the Medici Popes.

CHRIS

Say, Father, there's something I've been meaning to ask you. Do you know that sort of wing that's in back of the church over there? The red brick one, I mean.
(pointing in direction)

DEAN

St Mike's.

Yeah, right. St Mike's. What goes on in there, Father?

DEAN

Oh, that's where we say Black Mass.

CHRIS
(as Perrin chuckles)

What's that?

PERRIN

Oh, he's kidding.

CHRIS

I wasn't. I'd still like to know what it is.

DEAN

Oh, well, basically, I guess, it's a travesty of the Catholic
Mass. It's connected to witchcraft. Devil worship cults.
(looking around for someone)
Gee, where's Joe? He knows all about this stuff.

*He is indicating Father Dyer, who is standing at the buffet, heaping a
second helping on to his plate.*

Hey, Joe!

DYER
(turning)

You called, Great Dean?

Dean beckons him over.

DEAN
(to Chris)

They had a couple of cases of desecration in Holy Trinity last
week, and Joe said something about one of them reminding
him of some things they used to do at Black Mass, so I expect
he knows something about the subject.

PERRIN

What happened at the church?

DEAN

Oh, it's really too disgusting.

DYER

Listen, give me just a minute. I think I've got something going over there with the astronaut.

DEAN

What?

DYER
(*raising eyebrows*)
First missionary on the moon?

They burst into laughter as he moves off to join the Astronaut.

CHRIS

He's fun.
(*to Dean*)
You haven't told me what goes on yet in back of St Mike's. Big secret? Who's that priest I keep seeing there? You know, sort of dark? Do you know the one I mean?

DEAN
(*lowered tone, trace of regret*)
Father Karras.

CHRIS

What's he do?

DEAN

He's our counselor, Chris. A psychiatrist. The back of St Mike's is our couch.

CHRIS

Oh, I see.

DEAN

Had a pretty rough knock last night, poor guy. His mother passed away.

CHRIS
(*sensation of grief*)
Oh, I'm sorry.

DEAN

He seems to be taking it pretty hard. She was living by herself,

45

and I guess she was dead for a couple of days before they found her.

PERRIN
(*murmur*)
Oh, how awful.

DEAN
The superintendent of her apartment building found her at four in the morning. They wouldn't have found her even then except . . . Well, the next-door neighbors complained about her radio going all the time.

Two shot. Dyer and Astronaut. The Astronaut is breaking up as:

DYER
No, I'm really not a priest. I'm actually a terribly avant-garde rabbi.

INT. MACNEIL HOUSE. KITCHEN. NIGHT

Chris is bursting in as Dennings continues to rave at a stolid, expressionless Karl who stands immobile, arms akimbo, watching Dennings.

DENNINGS
Cunting *Hun*! You bloody damned butchering Nazi *pig*!

CHRIS
(*over Dennings*)
Karl! Will you get out of here! Get out!

Sharon enters now and Chris has started pushing Karl out. The latter, defiant, permits it only reluctantly.

DENNINGS
What the hell makes you think you're so fucking superior? Goddamned cunting Heinrich Himmler! Get the hell back to – !

Karl is out and now Dennings, in a remarkable performance, is instantly composed and as Chris turns to him after shoving Karl out of the door, Dennings turns to her genially and rubs his hands together with:

46

Now, then, what's dessert?

CHRIS

Des*sert*!

DENNINGS
(whining)

Well, I'm hungry.

Chris reacts, incredulous and exasperated, then turns and exits. Passing Sharon:

CHRIS

Feed him!

INT. REGAN'S BEDROOM. NIGHT

Regan is in bed. Chris is tucking her bedcovers in. The room lights are out and Regan is turned on her side. She has her eyes closed. Chris, finished, looks down at her.

CHRIS

You okay, hon?

No response. Chris waits. Regan appears to be asleep. Chris leans over, kisses her cheek.

(whisper)

Sleep tight.

INT. MACNEIL HOUSE. ANGLE AT MAIN STAIRCASE. NIGHT

Dyer and Dean are singing and playing, 'Oh, Lindberg (What a Flyin' Fool Was He)'. Camera goes to Chris holding the front door open for Sharon and the Assistant Director with a barely conscious Dennings being carried between them, heading for the open front door.

CHRIS

Night, Burke. Take it easy.

DENNINGS
(eyes still closed; a mutter)

Fuck it!

Chris shakes her head. Then the camera follows her to the piano group,

47

which now includes the Astronaut. Dyer is just finishing the song.
Group applauds. Dyer spots Chris.

DYER

Hi, Chris. Great party.

CHRIS

Thanks, Father. Keep goin'.

DYER
(playing chords)
I don't need the encouragement. My notion of heaven is a
solid white nightclub with me center stage for all the rest of
eternity.
(after amused reaction from group)
Does anyone else know the words to 'I'll Bet You're Sorry
Now, Tokyo Rose'.

*Chris starts singing as Dyer delightedly joins her. Then abruptly he
stops, staring expressionlessly at something off-screen. Chris, too, stops as
Dyer nods his head toward spot off-screen.*

I believe we have a visitor, Mrs MacNeil.

*On Chris and Astronaut. Chris looks where Dyer has indicated, and as
sudden silence falls on the group, Chris gasps in shock and dismay,
hand flying to her cheek, a small whimper coming up in her throat. The
camera moves to tight on the Astronaut's face as he, too, looks down
and we hear:*

REGAN
(off-screen)
You're going to die up there.

*As the Astronaut's face turns gray with dismay and chilling
apprehension, we hear:*

CHRIS
(off-screen; anguished)
Oh, my God! Oh, –

*Astronaut's POV: On Regan. Regan, in nightgown, is staring up at the
Astronaut (camera), and is urinating gushingly on to the rug.*

48

CHRIS
(*off-screen; continuing*)
– my God. Oh my baby!

The angle widens out to disclose Chris rushing up to Regan and leading her away toward the stairs.

Oh, come on, Rags, come with me, come upstairs!
(*over shoulder to the Astronaut*)
Oh, I'm so sorry! She's been sick, she must be walking in her sleep! She didn't know what she was saying!

Close on Astronaut, staring, shaken.

INT. REGAN'S BATHROOM. NIGHT

Regan sits in the tub like someone in a trance while Chris rapidly bathes her.

CHRIS
Honey, why did you say that? Why?

INT. REGAN'S BEDROOM. NIGHT

Moonlight streams in through open window. Regan, turned toward the wall, is in bed, dully staring at a point in space. Chris sits on edge of bed. Through the window, from the street below, we hear off-screen sounds and voices of departing guests.

CHRIS
Howya feelin', honey? Better?

No response.

Would you like me to read to you?

Regan shakes head slightly, still staring at the wall.

Okay, then. Try to sleep.

She leans over, kisses Regan, rises.

'Night, my baby.

49

Chris leaves and is almost out the door when she is arrested by Regan calling to her in a low, despairing, haunted tone:

> REGAN

Mother, what's wrong with me?

> CHRIS

Why, honey, it's nerves. That's all. I mean, it's just like the doctor said. You keep taking those pills and you'll be fine. Just fine.

A long wait for reaction, but Regan neither moves nor speaks.

Okay, Rags?

Chris waits. Still nothing. Troubled and despondent, Chris starts out of room.

INT. SECOND-FLOOR HALL OF MACNEIL HOUSE. NIGHT

The camera is fixed at one end of the hall, and we see Chris exit at the other from Regan's bedroom. Head down, thoughtful, she starts toward us; then remembers something and moves back to lean over the balustrade railing and observe something below for a moment or two. We hear off-screen a scraping sound, like a brush against carpeting: Willie brushing out the urine stains.

> CHRIS
> *(softly)*

Comin' out, Willie?

> WILLIE

Yes, madam. I think so.

> CHRIS
> *(slight nod)*

Good.

She continues to stare for a moment more, then comes toward the camera again until she reaches the door to her bedroom and enters. She closes the door. A beat. Then, from off-screen, within Regan's bedroom, we hear metallic sounds, like bedsprings violently quivering. They are tentative at first, then insistent. Then:

REGAN

(*off-screen; calling with burgeoning apprehension and surmise*)
Mother?

Two beats. The bedspring sounds. Then, much louder, and filled with terror:

(*off-screen*)

Mother, come *here*! Come *here*!

Chris's door has already shot open, and she's burst out into the hall, racing for Regan's bedroom.

CHRIS

Yes, I'm coming! All right, hon! I'm coming!

REGAN

(*off-screen*)

Moththheerrrrrrr!

CHRIS

Oh, my baby, what's –

INT. REGAN'S BEDROOM. DOOR. NIGHT

Chris bursts in, continuing as she reaches for the light switch and we hear massive metallic sounds now:

CHRIS

– wrong, hon? What is it? What's – ?

The lights are on, and as Chris stares at Regan's bed off-screen, she breaks off, electrified.

Jesus! Oh, Jesus!

POV: At Regan. She lies taut on her back, face stained with tears and contorted with terror and confusion as she grips the sides of the narrow bed. It is savagely quivering back and forth!

REGAN

Mother, why is it *shaking*? Make it stop! Oh, I'm scared! Make it stop! Oh, I'm scared, Mother, please make it stooooooooooo –

51

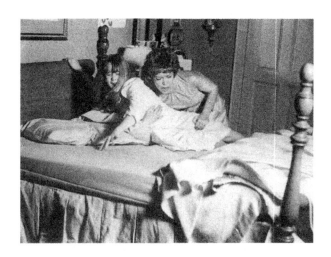

*And on her elongated, fearful cry, we break it off before the 'p' sound as
we:*

CUT TO:

INT. JESUIT RESIDENCE HALL. NIGHT

Dyer enters.

INT. CORRIDOR IN RESIDENCE HALL. NIGHT

Follow Dyer to Karras's room.

INT. KARRAS'S ROOM. NIGHT

*Dim desk-lamp lighting. Dyer sits back of Karras's desk wearing a
Snoopy T-shirt. Karras is sitting on the edge of his cot, his eyes fixed low
in a haunted stare. They are red and raw from weeping. In his hand is
a cup containing a small amount of Scotch, and his eyes and voice are
fogged by heavy drinking and chronic sleeplessness. Dyer is pouring from
a bottle of Chivas Regal into Karras's cup.*

KARRAS

Where'd you get the money for Chivas Regal, Joe? The
poorbox?

DYER

Don't be an asshole, that would be breaking my vow of
poverty.

KARRAS

Where did you get it then?

DYER

I stole it.

KARRAS

I believe you.

DYER

College presidents shouldn't drink. It tends to set a bad
example. I figure I relieved him of a terrible temptation.

Karras is nodding slightly, smiling, when suddenly he bursts into sobs.

KARRAS

Ah, Joe.

DYER
(with comforting gestures)

I know. I know.

Karras cries it through, the sobbing gradually subsiding.

KARRAS
(a whisper)

Ah, God.

*Karras at last exhales an enormous sigh, closing his eyes, outstretched on
the cot.*

DYER

Do you think you can sleep now, Damien?

*Karras nods his head along with a throat sound of affirmation. Dyer
moves to the foot of the bed, undoes laces and removes Karras's shoes.*

KARRAS

Gonna steal my shoes now?

DYER

No, I tell fortunes by reading the creases. Now shut up and go to sleep.

KARRAS

You're a Jesuit cat-burglar.

DYER

Listen, someone's got to worry about the bills around this place.

(*moving softly to desk*)

All you other guys do is just rattle your beads and pray for the hippies down on 'M' Street.

Dyer flicks off the desk light.

KARRAS

Stealing is a sin.

A beat. Then, tenderly, Dyer touches a hand to Karras's shoulder in good night, but as he starts to move toward the door, Karras's hand reaches out and grips Dyer's wrist, squeezing, and giving a little shake in a gesture of gratitude and deep friendship. At this moment, the camera is tight on the hands, but then goes to Dyer, as he nods in acknowledgement. Then Dyer stares down and the camera follows his gaze to tight at the hands again, as healing sleep at last comes to Karras and his grip slackens and his hand falls.

DYER

(*off-screen; whisper*)

Good night, Damien.

INT. HOLY TRINITY CHURCH. VERY EARLY MORNING

Only two or three Worshippers in the church. Karras, in his black vestments, is at the main altar saying Mass. While washing hands at a small table to the side of the altar:

KARRAS

O Lord, I have loved the beauty of Thy house and the place

54

where Thy glory dwelleth. Take not away my soul, O God, with the wicked, nor my life with men of blood . . .

Another angle. (Time lapse.) Now Karras's eyes are moistening with tears as:

Remember also, O Lord, Thy servant, Mary Karras . . . who has gone before us with the sign of faith, and sleeps the sleep of peace. To her, O Lord, and to – all –
                    (*he's fighting tears*)
– who rest in Christ, grant her – we pray Thee, a place of – refreshment – of light – and . . .
                    (*striking his breast*)
To us also, Thy sinful servants . . .

Another angle. (Time lapse.)

Peace I leave you; my peace I give you. Look not upon my sins but upon the faith of your church . . .

Another angle. (Time lapse.)

                    (*hands extended*)
O Lord, I am not worthy. Speak but the word and my soul shall be healed.

INT. DR KLEIN'S EXAMINING-ROOM. DAY

While Klein attempts to administer an injection, Chris and Nurse forcibly restrain a struggling, kicking Regan who is shrieking as:

                    CHRIS
Please, honey! It's to *help* you!

                    REGAN
I don't *want* it! I don't – !

Klein leans over, injects needle.

Son of a bitch *bastard*!

She spits in Klein's face.

INT. HALL OF DR KLEIN'S SUITE OF OFFICES. DAY

                    KLEIN
Well, it's sometimes a symptom of a type of disturbance in
the chemico-electrical activity of the brain. In the case of your
daughter, in the temporal lobe.
               (*a hand to side of his skull*)
Up here, in the lateral part of the brain. Now it's rare, but it
does cause bizarre hallucinations and usually happens just
before a convulsion. It –

                    CHRIS
               (*frowning over the 'it'*)
Convulsion.

                    KLEIN
               (*faintly evasive*)
Well, the shaking of the bed. That was doubtless due to
muscular spasms.

                    CHRIS
To muscular spasms? Hey, I was on the bed and it even
shook with me on it.

                    KLEIN
Look, Mrs MacNeil – your daughter's problem isn't her bed.
It's in her brain.

                    CHRIS
Yeah, okay. So what causes this . . .?
               (*she can't find the term*)

                    KLEIN
Lesion of the temporal lobe. It's a kind of . . . well, seizure
disorder.

                    CHRIS
Yeah. Look, I'll tell you the truth, Doc; I don't understand
how her whole personality could change.

                    KLEIN
In temporal lobe, that's very common, and can last in some
cases for several days. It isn't rare to find destructive, even
criminal behavior.

56

Chris closes her eyes and lowers her forehead on to a fist.

> **CHRIS**
> *(murmuring)*
> Listen, tell me somethin' good.

> **KLEIN**
> Well, now, don't be alarmed. If it's a lesion, in a way, she's
> fortunate. Then all we have to do is remove the scar.

INT. RADIOLOGICAL LAB. DAY

*Series of shots. Regan having her brain X-rayed (arteriogram). Chris
and Radiologist present.*

CUT TO:

INT. SMALL MEDICAL LAB AND X-RAY ROOM. DAY

*We begin close on the X-ray of Regan's skull, then disclose Klein and a
consulting neurologist (Dr Tanney) thoughtfully studying several of them.*

*Tanney, shaking his head, removes his eyeglasses and tucks them into
the breast pocket of his jacket with:*

> **TANNEY**
> There's just nothing there. No vascular distortion at all.

> **KLEIN**
> *(frowning, still studying X-rays)*
> Doesn't figure.

> **TANNEY**
> Want to run another series?

> **KLEIN**
> *(turning away from X-rays)*
> I don't think so.

We hear telephone buzzer simultaneous with:

> *(picking up wall phone)*
> I'd like you to see her again.
> *(into phone)*
> Yes.

57

RECEPTIONIST'S VOICE
(*urgent phone*)
Chris MacNeil's on the line! Says it's urgent!

INT. MACNEIL HOUSE. SECOND-FLOOR HALL. DAY

The camera is by the door to Regan's bedroom, from which emanate Regan's moans of pain and screams of terror. Rushing up from steps on the landing is Sharon, followed by Klein and Tanney. At the door, Sharon cracks it open and calls in:

SHARON

Chris, Doctors!

Chris immediately comes to the door, opening it. She is extremely distraught and bewildered.

INT. REGAN'S BEDROOM DOOR. DAY

Karl stands beside the door, staring numbly at off-screen sounds, and as the doctors enter, we hear the off-screen sound of something slamming on to bedsprings repeatedly (in addition to Regan's cries).

REGAN
(*off-screen; hysterical wail*)
Mooooootheeeeerrrrr!

POV: On Regan flailing her arms; her body seems to be flinging itself up horizontally about a foot into the air above her bed, and then is slammed down savagely on to the mattress, as if by an unseen person, and causing wrenching of Regan's breath. It happens repeatedly and rapidly as:

Oh, Mother, make him stop! Please *stop* him! *Stop* him! He's trying to kill me! He's – ! Oh, please stoopppppppppp himmmmmmmmmmm, Motherrrrrrrrrrrrr!

On Chris and doctors.

CHRIS
Doc, what *is* it? What's *happening*?

He shakes his head, gaze fixed on Regan.

POV: on Regan. The up-and-down movements briefly; then they
abruptly cease, and Regan twists feverishly from side to side, her eyes
rolling upwards, into their sockets so that only the whites are exposed,
while her legs keep crossing and uncrossing rapidly.

REGAN
(*moaning*)
Oh, he's burning me! I'm burning! I'm –! *Uhh!*

With this sudden sound of pain, Regan has abruptly jerked her head
back, disclosing a bulging, swollen throat, and she begins to mutter
incomprehensibly in a strangely deepened, guttural tone.

Another angle as the doctors approach. Reaching the bedside, Klein
reaches down to take Regan's pulse.

KLEIN
(*soothingly*)
All right, now let's see what the trouble is, dear. I'm just
going to –

And abruptly Klein is reeling, stunned and staggering, across the room
from the force of a vicious backward swing of Regan's arm as she
suddenly sits up, her face contorted with hideous rage. Now, in a coarse
and powerful, deep male voice:

REGAN
The sow is *mine! Mine!* Keep *away* from her!

On Klein. He stares off-screen, stunned, as Karl and Tanney kneel to
his assistance.

KLEIN
I'm all right.

They look toward Regan as we hear from off-screen a yelping laugh
gushing up in her throat.

On Regan. Her head is tilted back. The laugh continues, demonic.
Then she falls to her back as if someone has pushed her down. She pulls
back her nightgown with:

REGAN
Fuck me, fuck –

On Regan. Sitting up, she begins to caress her own arms sensually as she croons in that guttural, coarse, male voice:

Ah, my flower . . . my pearl . . .

Abruptly she falls on to her back again as if from a shove, and cries out with a wrench of breath. Then abruptly she is sitting up again, as if pulled by the hands, and:

(*normal voice*)
Oh, Mother! Mother – !

Another sudden cry, and then she is bending at the waist, whirling her torso around in rapid, strenuous circles.

(*weeping*)
Oh, *stop* him, please *stop* him! It hurts! Make him *stop*! Make him *stop*! I can't breaaaaaaathe!

On Chris.

CHRIS

Oh, my God, oh, my – !

On Regan. Before she finishes her cry, she again appears to be shoved savagely on to her back, and as Tanney comes beside the bed and observes, her eyes roll upward into their sockets and again she begins muttering incomprehensibly in that thickened voice. Tanney leans closer to try to make it out, frowning.

On Klein. He is by the large window overlooking steps, preparing a hypodermic injection.

KLEIN

Sam!

He beckons Tanney over to him with a move of the head and continues preparing the hypodermic. We hear the off-screen, fevered gibberish from Regan. Tanney comes into frame.

I'm giving her Librium. You're going to have to hold her.

They look quickly toward:

REGAN
(off-screen; terrified)
Oh, no! No! No! Captain Howdy, – !

Regan slamming up and down off the bed again.

Mother! Mother! Motherrrrrrrr!

QUICK CUT TO:

On Chris. Over Regan's prolonged scream of pain and terror, Chris, with fists to her temples, turns to shriek at doctors:

CHRIS
God almighty, will you *do* something! Help her! Help – !

On doctors. Klein is ready. And over:

(off-screen; continuing)
– herrrrrrrrrrrrrrr . . . !

and Regan's continuing scream from off-screen, Klein grimly nods to Tanney. And as they start toward bed with both Chris and Regan's cries persisting we

QUICK CUT TO:

INT. MACNEIL HOUSE. SECOND-FLOOR HALL. DAY

Blessed silence. Chris and Sharon have heads lowered waiting by the balustrade. Klein and Tanney exit Regan's room and approach them. Chris dabs at her nose with a moist, balled-up handkerchief, her eyes red from crying.

KLEIN
She's heavily sedated. She'll undoubtedly sleep right through until tomorrow.

CHRIS
Doc, how could she jump off the bed like that?

TANNEY
There's a perfectly rational explanation. Technically speaking, pathological states can induce abnormal strength and accelerated motor performance. You know the story – a

61

ninety-pound woman sees her child pinned under the wheel
of a truck, runs out and lifts the wheels half a foot up off the
ground. Same thing here.

CHRIS

Yeah, okay.

TANNEY

Same principle, I mean.

CHRIS

So what's wrong with her? What do you think?

KLEIN

Well, we still think it's temporal lobe, and –

CHRIS
(*erupting*)

What the hell are you talking about? She's been acting like
some kind of a psycho, like a split personality! What do you –
(*recovering*)

Guess I'm all uptight. I'm sorry. You were saying?

TANNEY

There haven't been more than a hundred authenticated cases of
so-called dual or split personality, Mrs MacNeil. Now I know
the temptation is to leap to psychiatry, but any reasonable
psychiatrist would exhaust the somatic possibilities first.

CHRIS

Okay, so what's next?

TANNEY

A pneumoencephelogram, I would think, to pin down that
lesion . . . outline the cavities of her brain. It *will* involve
another spinal.

CHRIS

Oh, Christ.

TANNEY

It's vital. What we missed in the EEG and the arteriograms
could conceivably turn up there. At the least, it would exhaust
certain other possibilities.

INT. MEDICAL LABORATORY. DAY

Lab Technician completes check of spinal fluid protein content.

INT. KLEIN'S OFFICE. DAY

Klein is looking at lab reports and seems baffled.

> KLEIN
> Dr Tanney says the X-rays are negative. In other words, normal.

Chris sighs, bowing head.

> CHRIS
> Well, –
>> *(bleak murmur)*
> here we are again, folks.

Klein stares down, shaking his head and frowning in perplexity. Then he looks up at Chris.

> KLEIN
> Do you keep any drugs in your house?

> CHRIS
> Huh?

> KLEIN
> Amphetamines? LSD?

> CHRIS
> Gee, no. Look, I'd tell you. No, there's nothing like that.

Klein nods and stares at his shoes; then looks up again.

> KLEIN
> Are you planning to be home soon? LA, I mean.

> CHRIS
> No. No, I'm building a new house and the old one's been sold. We were going to Europe for a while after Rags finished up with her school here. Why'd you ask?

> KLEIN
> I think it's time we started looking for a psychiatrist.

EXT. CHRIS'S CAR. NIGHT

As she drives back across Key Bridge.

INT. CHRIS'S CAR. NIGHT

Angle from driver's seat – 'M' Street and 36th. Through the windshield, dead ahead, a crowd has gathered by the base of the steep steps beside the house, and an ambulance is pulling out into traffic. White-coated Medics are running around in a panic. Police car lights are flashing. As Chris rounds off the bridge on to Prospect, the ambulance pulls out and gets just ahead of her, siren wailing. We follow the ambulance for two beats, then:

CUT TO:

EXT. MACNEIL HOUSE. REGAN'S WINDOW – CURTAINS BLOWING.
NIGHT

INT. MACNEIL HOUSE FRONT DOOR. NIGHT

Chris enters despondently. Closing door behind her, she leans back against it, looking down in thought, her hand still clutching the doorknob. A beat. The lights in the house blink out for a beat. Chris looks up. They blink out again, this time longer.

CHRIS

Sharon?

The lights come back on.

Shar?

Still no response. Chris starts up the staircase, frowning apprehensively.

INT. MACNEIL HOUSE. SECOND-FLOOR HALL. NIGHT

The camera is fixed by the door to Regan's bedroom. As Chris reaches the landing, the lights blink out again, briefly, then on. Chris has halted, her eyes warily scanning around, then she continues down the hall toward us, and opens the door to Regan's bedroom.

INT. REGAN'S BEDROOM. NIGHT

Full shot. Silence as Chris stands by the door a moment; then she goes to Regan's bedside, and rubs at her arms, as if from extreme cold. She examines Regan, who is still sound asleep.

Closer angle on Chris hugging herself, shivering.

> CHRIS
> (*perplexed; whisper*)

Shit!

Then she looks toward window; frowns in consternation.

The room. Full shot. The window is open. Chris moves to it and stares for a moment. She closes and locks it. But she still feels cold. She hears the front door opening from off-screen, below, through the open door to Regan's bedroom, and turns toward the sound. We follow her out into:

INT. MACNEIL HOUSE. SECOND-FLOOR HALL. NIGHT

As Chris exits and softly closes Regan's door. She starts toward stairs.

> CHRIS
> (*calling softly*)

Sharon?

INT. MACNEIL HOUSE. FOYER. LIVING-ROOM AREA. NIGHT

Sharon enters the house with a white paper pharmacy bag in hand.

> CHRIS

Hey, what the hell's wrong with you, Sharon? You go out and leave Rags by herself? Where've you been?

> SHARON

Oh, didn't he tell you?

> CHRIS

Oh, didn't *who* tell me?

> SHARON

Burke. Isn't he here? Where is he?

CHRIS

He was here?

SHARON

You mean he wasn't when you got home?

CHRIS

Listen, start all over.

SHARON

Oh, that nut. I couldn't get the druggist to deliver. Karl and Willie are off, so when Burke came around, I thought, fine, he can stay here with Regan while I go get the Thorazine. Guess I should have known.

CHRIS

Yeah, you should've.

SHARON

What happened with the tests?

CHRIS

Not a thing. I'm going to have to get Regan a shrink.

INT. FOYER AREA OF MACNEIL HOUSE. NIGHT

Chris is answering the door. It is the Assistant Director, ashen-faced.

CHRIS

Oh, Chuck. How ya doin'? Come on in.

ASSISTANT DIRECTOR
(*stepping inside gravely*)

You haven't heard?

CHRIS

Heard what?

Sharon enters scene, listening.

ASSISTANT DIRECTOR

Well, it's bad.

CHRIS

What's bad?

Burke's dead.

CHRIS

Oh, no!

SHARON

What happened?

ASSISTANT DIRECTOR

I guess he was drunk. He fell down from the top of the steps
right outside. By the time he hit 'M' Street, he'd broken his
neck.

Chris puts a hand to her mouth stifling a sob.

Yeah, I know.

(exiting)

See you later.

*He closes door behind him. Chris leans against door crying while
Sharon moves despondently to the foot of the staircase.*

CHRIS

Oh, Burke! Poor Burke!

SHARON

I can't believe it.

*Chris lowers her brow into her hand, leaning against the door. She
shakes her head, exhales.*

CHRIS

I guess everything –

*She breaks off, staring with horror at something descending the stairs
behind Sharon. It is Regan on all fours. She is gliding, spiderlike,
noiselessly and swiftly, down the staircase, her tongue flicking rapidly in
and out of her mouth like a snake. She halts directly beside Sharon.*

(numbly)

Sharon?

*Sharon stops, as does Regan. Sharon turns and sees nothing; and then
screams as she feels Regan's tongue snaking out at her ankle.*

67

Call that doctor and get him the hell over here, Sharon! Get
him *now*!

INT. RECEPTION AREA. DISTRICT MORGUE. DAY

*A young Attendant has his feet propped up on a desk. He is munching
at a sandwich while working a newspaper crossword puzzle. He looks
up off-scene at:*

*Police Detective Kinderman, a portly, middle-aged man; he shows his
ID.*

                    KINDERMAN
Dennings.

INT. MORGUE AREA. DAY

*Kinderman and the Attendant walk down between the banks of metal
lockers used for the filing of sightless eyes. They stop at the other end
where the Attendant finds the proper locker and then pulls it out full
length. Kinderman removes his hat, staring down.*

KINDERMAN

Pull the sheet back.

Up angle on Kinderman and the morgue Attendant, as the Attendant leans over and we hear the rustling sound of the sheet being pulled back. Never changing his expression, Kinderman mutely shakes his head.

ATTENDANT

Could that have happened from the fall?

KINDERMAN

Only from the one at the beginning of time.

INT. CHRIS'S BEDROOM. DAY

Shutters are closed and the room is dark. Klein stands by the bureau, watching. Chris sits on the edge of the bed, as does a Psychiatrist. He is swinging a bauble on a chain back and forth, hypnotically, in front of Regan. He shines a penlight on the bauble so that it glows in the dark. He halts, inclining the penlight beam up, and we see Regan's eyes are closed and she appears to be in a trance. He turns off the penlight.

PSYCHIATRIST

Are you comfortable, Regan?

REGAN

(voice soft and whispery)

Yes.

PSYCHIATRIST

How old are you?

REGAN

Twelve.

PSYCHIATRIST

Is there someone inside you?

REGAN

Sometimes.

PSYCHIATRIST

Who is it?

REGAN

I don't know.

PSYCHIATRIST

Captain Howdy?

REGAN

I don't know.

PSYCHIATRIST

If I ask *him* to tell me, will you let him answer?

REGAN

No!

PSYCHIATRIST

Why not?

REGAN

I'm afraid!

PSYCHIATRIST

If he talks to me, I think he will leave you. Do you want him to leave you?

REGAN

Yes.

PSYCHIATRIST

Let him speak, then. Will you let him speak?

REGAN
(*a pause; then:*)

Yes.

PSYCHIATRIST
(*firmly; new tone*)

I am speaking to the person inside of Regan, now. If you are there you too are hypnotized and must answer all my questions. Come forward and answer me now. Are you there?

No response, and after three beats, we hear Regan's breath coming loud and raspily, like a rotted, putrid bellows. The Psychiatrist sniffs, as if at a horrid smell, and then flicks on a laser lamp and shines it up into Regan's face. Chris gasps. We do not see Regan's face, but play off

70

reactions of Chris and the Psychiatrist. Chris lowers her head into a
hand, the sight too unbearable for her, and she grips the Psychiatrist's
arm with the other in a tight vise. This causes him to extinguish the
laser lamp.

Are you the person inside of Regan?

REGAN
(in the coarse and guttural voice)

Say.

PSYCHIATRIST

Did you answer?

REGAN

Say.

PSYCHIATRIST

If that's yes, nod your head.

Regan nods.

Who are you?

REGAN

Nowonmai.

PSYCHIATRIST

That's your name?

REGAN

Say.

PSYCHIATRIST

Are you speaking in a foreign language?

REGAN

Say.

PSYCHIATRIST

Are you someone whom Regan has known?

REGAN

One.

71

PSYCHIATRIST

That she knows of?

REGAN

One.

PSYCHIATRIST

Part of Regan?

REGAN

One.

PSYCHIATRIST

Do you like her?

REGAN

One.

PSYCHIATRIST

Do you hate her?

REGAN

Say.

PSYCHIATRIST

Are you punishing her?

REGAN

Say.

PSYCHIATRIST

You wish to harm her?

REGAN

Say.

PSYCHIATRIST

To kill her?

REGAN

Say.

PSYCHIATRIST

But if Regan died, wouldn't you die, too?

REGAN

One.

PSYCHIATRIST

Is there something she can do to make you leave her?

REGAN

Say.

PSYCHIATRIST

Do you blame her for her parents' divorce?

His question elides into a prolonged gasp of startled pain and horrified incredulity as we go quickly to full at Regan, mad, evil glee in the eyes as now the light drops from the Psychiatrist's hand.

Close on Psychiatrist. In the darkness, we see his mouth agape in horrible pain, his eyes wide-staring. What has happened is that Regan has gripped his scrotum in a hand that is squeezing like an iron talon.

PSYCHIATRIST

Marc! Marc, help me!

Quickly on Chris leaping up and away from the Psychiatrist struggling to wrench Regan's hand away, a hand with incredible strength.

CHRIS

Jesus!

Klein races forward toward the bed; Chris is running, panicked, for the light switch; Psychiatrist, in agony, struggling; Regan 'creature' with head tilted back is cackling demoniacally and then howls like a wolf as Chris slaps at the light switch. The lights come on and we see:

On bed. Regan, cackling demoniacally, is rolling around on the bed in savage struggle with Klein and Psychiatrist, who are still attempting to dislodge her hand from its grip. Grimaces. Gasps. Curses. The bedstead is quivering violently from side to side.

Another angle. Regan jerks upright. Her eyes roll upward into their sockets and she wrenches up a keening shriek of terror torn raw and bloody from the base of her spine as her face becomes her own. Then she falls backwards in a faint.

View of bed. Stillness. Regan unconscious. Two beats. One of the doctors makes a small move at extricating himself from the tangle. Chris crumples in a dead faint.

EXT. OUTDOOR TRACK IN HOLLOW OF GEORGETOWN UNIVERSITY
CAMPUS. DAY

In shorts and T-shirt, Karras is running laps. Parked on the road near the track is a police squad car, and seated on a bench at the edge of the track, watching Karras, is Kinderman. From off-screen the sounds of football practice. Karras seems curious, if not disturbed, by Kinderman's presence. When Karras slows to a walk, hands on hips, head down, panting, Kinderman rises and moves to catch up with him.

KINDERMAN
(calling)

Father Karras?

Karras turns, squinting into the sun, his breath coming in great gulps. He waits for Kinderman to reach him, then beckons him to follow as Karras resumes his walk.

KARRAS

Do you mind? I'll cramp.

KINDERMAN

Yes, of course.

KARRAS

Have we met?

KINDERMAN

No, we haven't, but they said I could tell; that you looked like a boxer. Some priest from the barracks. I forget. I'm so terrible, awful with names.

(flashing ID)

I'm William F. Kinderman, Father.

KARRAS

'Homicide'. What's this about?

74

You know, you *do* look like a boxer. Excuse me, but that scar
there by your eye? Just exactly Marlon Brando, it looks, in *On
the Waterfront*. People ever tell you that, Father?

KARRAS

People tell you that you look like Paul Newman?

KINDERMAN

Always. Incidentally, you're busy? I'm not interrupting?

KARRAS

Interrupting what?

KINDERMAN

Well, mental prayer, perhaps.

KARRAS
(*stopping*)

Is this about the desecrations?

KINDERMAN

Excuse me?

Karras gives him a skeptical look, then moves on, shaking his head.

Ah, well. A psychiatrist. Who am I kidding? I'm sorry, it's a habit with me, Father. Schmaltz. That's the Kinderman method.

KARRAS
(stopping)

Look, Lieutenant, if you want a sick priest, I can help you. I suggest you take a look in the Jesuit Infirmary and at one of the Jebbies there who's ninety years old and is convinced the Holy Spirit keeps hiding his socks to test his faith in the underlying order of the universe.

(moving on)

Thank you. That's the Damien Karras method.

KINDERMAN

People tell you for a priest you're a little bit smart-ass?

KARRAS

Always.

KINDERMAN

Maybe always isn't enough.

EXT. UNIVERSITY QUADRANGLE AREA. DAY

KINDERMAN

You know that director who was doing the film here, Father? Burke Dennings?

KARRAS

Yes, I've seen him.

KINDERMAN

You've seen him. You're familiar how he died?

KARRAS

Well, the papers . . .

KINDERMAN

No, the papers, that's just part of it. Part. Only part. Listen, what do you know on the subject of witchcraft, Father? From the witching end, please, not the hunting.

KARRAS

Well, I once did a paper on it.

KINDERMAN

Oh, really? Oh, that's wonderful! Great!

KARRAS
(drily)
You never knew that till this moment, I suppose.

KINDERMAN

Father, people can suppose what they want.

KARRAS

Go ahead.

KINDERMAN

It's a free country, Father.

KARRAS

Go *ahead.*

KINDERMAN

These desecrations . . . they remind you of anything to do
with witchcraft?

KARRAS

Maybe. Some rituals used in Black Mass.
(*stopping*)
What's that got to do with Dennings?

KINDERMAN

Burke Dennings, good Father, was found at the bottom of
those steps down to 'M' Street with his head turned
completely around and facing backwards.

Karras is floored; then he turns to meet Kinderman's steady gaze.

KARRAS

It didn't happen in the fall?

KINDERMAN

Oh, yes, it's possible . . . possible. However . . .

KARRAS

Unlikely.

Kinderman nods mutely. They resume walking.

KINDERMAN

And so what comes to mind in the context of witchcraft?

KARRAS

Well, supposedly, demons broke the necks of witches that
way.

KINDERMAN

They did. So, on the one hand, a murder, and on the other,
desecrations in the church identical with rituals used in devil
worship.

KARRAS

You think the killer and the desecrator are the same?

KINDERMAN

Maybe somebody crazy, Father Karras; maybe someone with
a spite against the Church, some unconscious rebellion,
perhaps.

INT. HEALY BUILDING. GROUND FLOOR. DAY

Karras and Kinderman are approaching us down the long hallway as:

KINDERMAN

And so who fits the bill, also lives in the neighborhood, knows
Latin, and also has access to the church in the night?

KARRAS

Sick priest.

KINDERMAN

Listen, Father, this is hard for you – please, I understand. But
for priests on the campus here, you're the psychiatrist; you'd
know who was sick at the time, who was not. I mean, *this* kind
of sickness. You'd know that.

KARRAS

Look, I really know of no one who fits the description.

KINDERMAN

Ah, of course, doctor's ethics. If you knew, you wouldn't tell.

KARRAS

No, I wouldn't.

KINDERMAN

Incidentally – and I mention it only in passing – this ethic at
the moment is maybe illegal. Not to bother you with trivia
and legal minutiae, but lately a psychiatrist in sunny
California was thrown into jail for not telling the police what
he knew about a patient.

KARRAS
(*slight smile*)

That a threat?

KINDERMAN

Don't talk paranoid, Father. I mention it only in passing.

KARRAS

I mention it only in passing, but I could always tell the judge
it was a matter of confession.

KINDERMAN

Want to go into business, Father? What 'Father'? You're a
Jew who's trying to pass; though, let me tell you, I think
you've gone a little bit far.

HEALY BUILDING. TOP OF STEPS. DAY

*Kinderman and Karras are coming through doors to the top of the steps
overlooking the entry circle, the front gates, the squad car below.*

KINDERMAN

Listen, Father. Listen, *doctor*. Am I crazy? Could there maybe
be a witch coven here in the District? Right now, I mean?
Today?

KARRAS

I don't know.

KINDERMAN
(*linking arms with Karras*)
Come on, we'll take you where you're going.

KARRAS
That's all right, thanks. It's just a short walk.

KINDERMAN
Never mind. Enjoy. You can tell all your friends you went
riding in a squad car.

KARRAS
Been there, done that.

Kinderman shakes his head ruefully.

EXT. GEORGETOWN STREET. SQUAD CAR. DAY

The car pulls up to the Jesuit Residence Hall and parks.

INT. SQUARD CAR. KARRAS AND KINDERMAN. DAY

KINDERMAN
You like movies, Father Karras?

KARRAS
Yes, I do.

KINDERMAN
I get passes for the very best shows. I always hate to go alone.
You know, I love to talk film; to discuss, to critique. Would
you like to see a movie with me sometime, Father? I've got
passes for the Biograph this week. It's *Othello*.

KARRAS
Who's in it?

KINDERMAN
Who's *in it*?

KARRAS
Yes, who's starring?

KINDERMAN

Debbie Reynolds, Desdemona, and Othello, Groucho Marx.
You're happy? What's the difference who's starring, who's
not?

KARRAS

I've seen it.

KINDERMAN

You are difficult, Father.

KARRAS

Yes.

As Karras is about to exit, Kinderman grabs his arm.

KINDERMAN

Listen, one more time: Can you think of some priest who fits
the bill?

KARRAS

Oh, come on, now!

KINDERMAN

Just answer the question, please, Father Paranoia.

KARRAS

Look, you want me to tell you who I really think did it?

KINDERMAN

Oh yes, who?

KARRAS

The Dominicans. Go pick on them.

KINDERMAN

I could have you deported, you know that?

KARRAS

What for?

KINDERMAN

A psychiatrist shouldn't piss people off. Plus also the goyim,
plainly speaking, would love it. Who needs it, a priest who
wears T-shirts and sneakers?

KARRAS

(smiling, exiting car)

Thanks a lot for the ride.

KINDERMAN

I lied! You look like Sal Mineo!

EXT. BARRINGER CLINIC. DAY

Establishing shot.

INT. ROOM IN BARRINGER CLINIC. DAY

Regan in another fit, in bed and restrained by straps. Clinic Director is in the room with other Doctors observing. They are baffled.

Hospital corridor. Nurse walking to the door to Regan's room. She pauses outside as she hears a curious rapping sound from within. She enters the room. Dim night-light illumination. The rappings have ceased. Regan is sleeping. Nurse checks her pulse, then frowns in wonderment as she spots something on Regan's chest. She parts Regan's pajama top to see better, and as she leans closer, she looks mystified. We now see that on Regan's chest, faintly, the letter 'L', followed by a separation, then the letter 'M', having risen up in blood-red, light bas-relief lettering on her skin.

INT. CLINIC DIRECTOR'S OFFICE. DAY

The room is glass enclosed on two sides, so that we have a view in the background of a traffic of doctors and nurses. Clinic Director and two of the Doctors from earlier clinic scenes are present. Chris sits in a chair, taut and drawn. In the room, a closed-circuit TV monitor showing Regan in the hospital room, in a fit, as:

CLINIC DIRECTOR

People with very, very sensitive skin can just trace with a finger, and then a little while later it shows up. Not abnormal. Why an 'L' and an 'M', of course, we don't understand. In the meantime . . .

Another angle. (*Time lapse.*)

It looks like a type of disorder that you rarely ever see any more, except among primitive cultures. We call it somnambuliform possession. Quite frankly, we don't know much about it except that it starts with some conflict or guilt that eventually leads to the patient's delusion that his body's been invaded by an alien intelligence; a spirit, if you will. In times gone by, the entity possessing the victim is supposed to be a so-called demon, or devil.

Full at TV monitor. (Time lapse.)

> CHRIS
>
> Look, I'm telling you again and you'd better believe it, I'm not about to put her in a goddamn asylum!

> CLINIC DIRECTOR
>
> It's –

> CHRIS
>
> I don't care *what* you call it! I'm not going to put her away!

> CLINIC DIRECTOR
>
> Well, I'm sorry.

> CHRIS
>
> Yeah, sorry. Christ, eighty-eight doctors and all you can tell me with all of your bullshit . . .

Another angle. (Time lapse.)

> CLINIC DIRECTOR
>
> There *is* one outside chance of a cure. I think of it as shock treatment. As I say, it's a *very* outside chance. But then since you're so opposed to your daughter being hospitalized –

> CHRIS
>
> Will you *name* it, for God's sake? What *is* it?

> CLINIC DIRECTOR
>
> Have you any religious beliefs?

> CHRIS
>
> No, I don't.

CLINIC DIRECTOR

And your daughter?

CHRIS

Why?

CLINIC DIRECTOR

Have you ever heard of exorcism, Mrs MacNeil?

CHRIS

Come again.

CLINIC DIRECTOR

It's a stylized ritual in which rabbis and priests try to drive out
a so-called invading spirit. It's pretty much discarded these
days, except by the Catholics who keep it in the closet as a
sort of embarrassment. It has worked, in fact, although not
for the reason they think, of course. It was purely the force of
suggestion. The victim's *belief* in possession helped cause it;
and in just the same way this belief in the power of exorcism
can make it disappear.

CHRIS

Are you telling me to take my daughter to a witch doctor?

EXT. STREET IN FRONT OF MACNEIL HOUSE. DAY

*Full shot. A limo has pulled up and Karl is exiting the driver's seat and
opening the rear door while Sharon exits on the right rear side. Karl
reaches in and picks up a small figure (Regan) wrapped in a blanket
from Chris in the back seat. While Karl carries Regan toward the door
of the MacNeil house where Willie is standing, anxiously watching,
Chris exits the car in deep depression.*

INT. REGAN'S BEDROOM. DAY

*Regan is faced to the side. Sharon is adjusting a Sustagen flask used for
a naso-gastric feeding. Karl is affixing a set of restraining straps to the
bed. Chris enters, stands by the door and observes. Karl lets the straps
hang loose, nods to Sharon. Sharon starts out of the room, pausing for a
moment by the door to look at Chris.*

Chris moves slowly forward to the bedside and looks down at Regan.

84

We see now that Regan's face is torn and bloated with numerous scratch marks and scabs. Projecting hideously from her nostrils is the naso-gastric tubing. Karl has finished adjusting the straps. He, too, now looks down at Regan. Two beats. He looks up at Chris.

> KARL

She is going to be well?

> CHRIS
> *(after a beat)*

I don't know.

Another angle. A beat. Then Chris leans and tenderly adjusts Regan's pillow. In the process, she discovers a crucifix under it made of white bone. She lifts it out, examining it, frowning. Then, at Karl:

Who put this crucifix under her pillow?

EXT. HOUSE. DAY

Camera behind Kinderman looking up to Regan's window.

INT. MACNEIL HOUSE. KITCHEN. DAY

Sharon, her coat still on, listless, sorts through a mound of mail and messages. Willie is slicing carrots for a stew. Chris enters with the crucifix.

> CHRIS
> *(to Sharon)*

Was it you put this under her pillow?

> SHARON
> *(fuddled)*

Whaddya mean?

> CHRIS

You didn't?

> SHARON

Chris, I don't even know what you're talking about. Listen, I told you . . .

CHRIS
(*interjecting*)

Yeah.

SHARON

All I've ever said to Rags is maybe 'God made the world', and
maybe things about –

CHRIS

Fine, Sharon. Fine. I believe you, but –

WILLIE

Me, I don't put it.

CHRIS

This fucking cross didn't just walk up there, dammit! Now –

She is interrupted by the entrance of Karl.

KARL

Please, madam, there is man here to see you.

CHRIS

What man?

INT. MACNEIL HOUSE. ENTRY HALL. DAY

*Kinderman stands waiting with hat in hand as Chris approaches. He
shows his ID.*

KINDERMAN

I'd know that face in *any* line-up, Mrs MacNeil.

CHRIS

Am I in one?

INT. MACNEIL HOUSE. KITCHEN. DAY

*Chris and Kinderman. On the breakfast table sits Regan's sculpt of the bird.
It is set among the salt and pepper shakers and is now a decorative piece.*

KINDERMAN
(*to Chris*)

Might your daughter remember if perhaps Mr Dennings was
in her room that night?

CHRIS

(*vague apprehensiveness*)

Why do you ask?

KINDERMAN

Might your daughter remember?

CHRIS

Oh, no, she was heavily sedated.

KINDERMAN

It's serious?

CHRIS

Yes, I'm afraid it is.

KINDERMAN

May I ask . . .?

CHRIS

We still don't know.

KINDERMAN

Watch out for drafts. A draft in the fall when a house is hot is a magic carpet for bacteria.

CHRIS

Why are you asking all this?

KINDERMAN

Strange . . . strange . . . so baffling. The deceased comes to visit, stays only twenty minutes without even seeing you, and leaves all alone here a very sick girl. And speaking plainly, Mrs MacNeil, as you say, it's not likely he would fall from a window. Besides that, a fall wouldn't do to his neck what we found except maybe a chance in a thousand. My hunch? My opinion? I believe he was killed by a powerful man: point one. And the fracturing of his skull – point two – plus the various things I have mentioned, would make it very probable – probable, not certain – the deceased was killed and then afterwards pushed from your daughter's window. But no one was here except your daughter. So how could this be? It could be one way: if someone came calling between the time Miss Spencer left and the time you returned.

CHRIS

(hoarsely; stunned)

Judas Priest, just a second.

KINDERMAN

The servants? They have visitors?

CHRIS

Never. Not at all.

KINDERMAN

You expected a package that day? Some delivery?

CHRIS

Not that I know of.

KINDERMAN

Dry-cleaning, maybe? Groceries? Liquor? A package?

CHRIS

I really wouldn't know. Karl handles all of that.

KINDERMAN

Oh, I see.

CHRIS

Want to ask him?

KINDERMAN

Never mind, it's remote. You've got a daughter very sick, and
– well, never mind.

Chris rises.

CHRIS

Would you like another cup of coffee?

Kinderman acknowledges in the affirmative.

INT. MACNEIL KITCHEN. DAY

*Kinderman follows Chris toward Sharon's working area. He notices
Regan's artwork.*

KINDERMAN

Cute . . . It's so cute. Your daughter. She's the artist?

Chris nods.

Incidentally, just a chance in a million, I know; but your
daughter – you could possibly ask her if she saw Mr Dennings
in her room that night?

CHRIS

Look, he wouldn't have a reason to be up there in the first
place.

KINDERMAN

I know that. I realize; that's true, very true. But if certain
British doctors never asked 'What's this fungus?' we wouldn't
today have penicillin. Correct?

CHRIS

When she's well enough, I'll ask.

KINDERMAN

Couldn't hurt. In the meantime . . .
        (*at the front door Kinderman falters, embarrassed*)
Look, I really hate to ask you; however . . .

CHRIS
(*tensing*)

What?

KINDERMAN
For my daughter . . . you could maybe give an autograph?

He has reddened, and Chris almost laughs with relief.

CHRIS
Oh, of course. Where's a pencil?

KINDERMAN
Right here!

He has whipped out the stub of a chewed-up pencil from the pocket of his coat while he dipped his other hand in a pocket of his jacket and slipped out a calling card.

She would love it.

CHRIS
What's her name?

Chris presses the card against the door and poises the pencil stub to write. There follows a weighty hesitation.

KINDERMAN
(*eyes desperate and defiant*)
I lied. It's for me.
(*fixes gaze on card and blushes*)
Write 'To William F. Kinderman' – it's spelled on the back.

Chris eyes him with a wan and unexpected affection, checks the spelling of his name and writes on the card as:

You know that film you made called *Angel*? I saw that film six times.

CHRIS
If you were looking for the murderer, arrest the director.

KINDERMAN
You're a very nice lady.

90

CHRIS

You're a very nice man.

*Kinderman exits. Chris leans against the door, thoughtful, for a
moment. Then she moves on.*

EXT. PROSPECT STREET. DAY

*About to enter police squad car, Kinderman notices it's parked in front
of a fire hydrant. He shakes his head.*

INT. SQUAD CAR. DAY

Kinderman enters, closes door, stares sourly at the Driver.

KINDERMAN

In front of a hydrant you parked?

DRIVER

I'm in the car.

KINDERMAN

So am I. Proving what? The existence of God or that the
hydrant isn't there? You're talking Zen.

*The Driver moves the car forward a few feet and it stops with a lurch.
Kinderman eyes the Driver dismally, then opens the glove compartment,
extracts an evidence envelope, scrapes out something from under his
fingernail – paint from the little sculpt he picked up in the MacNeil
house – hands it to the Driver. During this:*

And now take this to the lab for a spectrum analysis and have
them compare it with the paint from the desecrated statue in
the church.

INT. MACNEIL HOUSE. KITCHEN. DAY

*Chris enters, moves to counter, feels at coffee pot. It's cold. She takes her
hand away, stares down, pensive. Then, drawn by the sound of the
washing-machine, she looks up toward the open door to basement, then
moves to it. Calling down:*

CHRIS

Willie.

WILLIE

Oh, yes, madam.

CHRIS

Look, never mind dinner tonight. I'm not hungry, and if
anyone –

*Her eye has fallen to a book that is lying open, face down, on top of the
dryer. In an insert we see the title:* A History of Witchcraft. *Picking it
up:*

You reading this?

WILLIE

I try, but very difficult, madam.

CHRIS

Some illustrations.

WILLIE

I find in Miss Regan bedroom.

*Chris looks up at her. The dryer stops spinning and Willie turns away to
take out the clothes. Chris resumes thumbing through the book. Abruptly
she freezes, turning ashen. She holds the gaze on the book for a beat;
then, numbly:*

CHRIS

Willie – you found this in Regan's bedroom?

WILLIE

Yes, madam. Under bed.

*Still numb, Chris runs a finger along the edge of a right-hand page, and
in an insert, we see that a narrow strip – in the manner of Burke
Dennings – has been surgically shaved from along its length.*

*Another angle. Willie and Chris look up at a sound from above, in
Regan's bedroom, of a blow, of someone staggering across the room, of
someone crashing to the wall and falling heavily to the ground. This is
followed, as Chris races upstairs, by an at-first-indistinct altercation
between a tearful and terror-stricken Regan and someone else – a man –
with a powerful and incredibly deep bass voice. Regan is pleading; the
man commanding in obscene terms.*

Angle on Chris from top of steps (second floor). Rushing up, frenzied, while Willie and Sharon stare up from bottom of steps. We hear:

> REGAN
> *(off-screen)*
> No! Oh, no, don't! Don't – !

> MALE VOICE
> *(off-screen)*
> *Do* it, damned piglet! You'll – !

> REGAN
> *(off-screen)*
> No! Oh, no don't! Please, don't –

And in this manner, the voices continue – and never overlapping – while the camera tracks with Chris to the door to Regan's bedroom.

INT. REGAN'S BEDROOM. DAY

Chris bursts in, then stands rooted in shock, as we hear the sound of the bed shaking violently, and the continuation of dialogue between Regan and the thundering deep Male Voice.

> REGAN
> *(off-screen)*
> *Please!* Oh, please don't m[-ake] – !

> MALE VOICE
> *(off-screen)*
> You'll do as I tell you, filth! You'll – !

Chris has turned her head to stare at:

POV: On Karl. Blood trickling down from his forehead, he lies unconscious on the floor near the bureau. The camera goes to the bed disclosing Regan sitting up in a side view to camera, her legs propped wide apart and the bone-white crucifix clutched in raw-knuckled hands that are upraised over her head. She seems to be exerting a powerful effort to keep the crucifix up, away from her vagina, which we cannot (and will not) see, her nightgown pulled up to precisely that point. We see that her face alters expression to match each voice in the argument, both of which are coming from her! When the deep Male Voice speaks through her mouth, the features instantaneously contort into a demonic grimace of malevolence and rage. Blood trickles down from Regan's nose. The naso-gastric tubing has been ripped out. During the above:

REGAN

Oh, no don't make me! Don't!

REGAN/DEMON

You'll do it!

REGAN

No! No –!

REGAN/DEMON

Do it, stinking bitch! You'll do it! You'll do it or I'm going to kill you!

REGAN

Nooooo!

REGAN/DEMON

Yes, *do* it, *do* it, do –!

QUICK CUT TO:

Close down angle on Regan showing nothing from the waist down as with eyes wide and staring she seems to be flinching from the rush of some hideous finality, her mouth agape and shrieking in terror as she stares up at the upheld crucifix. Then the shriek ends as the demonic face once again takes over her features, and the piercing cry of terror elides into a yelping, guttural laugh of malevolent spite and rage triumphant as the crucifix is plunged down and out of sight at Regan's vagina. The demonic face looks down, and we hear Regan/Demon roaring in that coarse deafening voice as the crucifix is repeatedly brought up and plunged down again, blood now spotting it as:

REGAN/DEMON

Yes, now you're *mine*, you stinking cow! You're *mine*, you're *mine*, you're –!

Chris has raced in, screaming, grappling to take hold of the crucifix. We see blood on Regan's thighs, but never the vagina. The Demon first turns on Chris with a look of mindbending fury. Then:

94

Ahhh, little pig-mother!

*The Demon pulls Chris's head down, rubbing her face sensually against
the pelvic area, then lifts her head and smashes Chris a blow across the
chest that sends her reeling across the room and crashing to a wall with
stunning force while Demon laughs with bellowing spite. Chris crumples
against the wall near Karl. Willie arrives, staring in confusion and
horror. Chris begins to pick herself up. She stares toward the bed, her
face bloodied, and begins to crawl painfully toward it.*

Ah, there's my pearl, my sweet honey piglet!

*Chris's POV: Moving shot on bed as she crawls closer. Regan now has
her back to camera, looking down, and we know the crucifix is being
used for masturbation.*

Ah! Yes, mine, you are mine, you are – !

*It breaks off and Regan/Demon abruptly looks over her shoulder at
camera (and Chris), which halts at the sight. The features of Regan's
face seem to be those of Burke Dennings. Then it speaks in the British-
accented giggly voice of the dead director.*

REGAN/DENNINGS
Do you know what she *did*, your cunting daughter?

Close on Chris screaming in horror.

QUICK CUT TO:

EXT. 35TH STREET BRIDGE AND CANAL AREA. DAY

*Chris. She wears oversized dark glasses and is leaning over the bridge
railing.*

*Another angle as Chris sees a large, powerfully built man wearing
khakis, sweater and sturdy, scuffed white tennis shoes approaching her.
She quickly looks away. Though she doesn't recognize him, we see it is
Karras. Coming up beside her:*

KARRAS
Are you Chris MacNeil?

CHRIS
Keep movin', creep.

KARRAS
I'm Father Karras.

Chris reddens, jerks swiftly around.

CHRIS
Oh, my God! Oh, I'm – ! *Jesus!*

She is tugging at her sunglasses, flustered, and immediately pushing them back as the sad, dark eyes probe hers.

KARRAS
I suppose I should have told you that I wouldn't be in uniform.

CHRIS
Yeah, it would've been terrific. Got a cigarette, Father?

KARRAS
(reaching into pocket of shirt)
Sure.

Chris lights up. After a deep exhalation of smoke:

CHRIS
How'd a shrink ever get to be a priest?

KARRAS
It's the other way around. The Society sent me through medical school and psychiatric training.

CHRIS
Where?

KARRAS
Oh, well, Harvard, Johns Hopkins, Bellevue, then –

CHRIS
(over him)
You're a friend of Father Dyer's, that right?

KARRAS
Yes, I am.

CHRIS
Pretty close?

96

KARRAS

Pretty close.

CHRIS

Did he talk about the party?

KARRAS

Yes.

CHRIS

About my daughter?

KARRAS

No, I didn't know you had one.

CHRIS

Yeah, she's twelve. He didn't mention her?

KARRAS

No.

CHRIS

He didn't tell you what she did?

KARRAS

He never mentioned her.

CHRIS

Priests keep a pretty tight mouth, then. That right?

KARRAS

That depends.

CHRIS

On what?

KARRAS

On the priest.

CHRIS

I mean, what if a person, let's say, was a criminal, like maybe a murderer or something, you know? If he came to you for help, would you have to turn him in?

KARRAS

If he came to me for spiritual help, I'd say, no.

97

CHRIS

You wouldn't.

KARRAS

No, I wouldn't. But I'd try to persuade him to turn himself in.

CHRIS

And how do you go about getting an exorcism?

KARRAS

Beg pardon?

CHRIS

If a person's possessed by some kind of a demon, how do you go about getting an exorcism?

KARRAS

Well, first you'd have to put him in a time machine and get him back to the sixteenth century.

CHRIS
(*puzzled*)

Didn't get you.

KARRAS

Well, it just doesn't happen anymore, Miss MacNeil.

CHRIS

Since when?

KARRAS

Since we learned about mental illness, about paranoia, dual personality, all of those things that they taught me at Harvard.

CHRIS

You kidding?

KARRAS

Many educated Catholics, Miss MacNeil, don't believe in the devil anymore, and as far as possession is concerned, since the day I joined the Jesuits I've never met a priest who's ever in his life performed an exorcism. Not one.

CHRIS

Oh, really.

(*a shaking hand to her sunglasses*)

Well, it happens, Father Karras, that someone very close to me is probably possessed. She needs an exorcism. Will you do it?

She has slipped off the glasses and Karras feels momentary, wincing shock at the redness, at the desperate pleading in the haggard eyes.

Father Karras, it's my *daughter!*

KARRAS

(*gently*)

Then all the more reason to forget about exorcism and –

CHRIS

(*outburst in a cracking voice*)

Why? God, I don't under*stand!*

Karras takes her wrist in a comforting hand.

KARRAS

To begin with it could make things worse.

CHRIS

But *how?*

KARRAS

The ritual of exorcism is dangerously suggestive. And secondly, Miss MacNeil, before the Church approves an exorcism, it conducts an investigation to see if it's warranted. That takes time. In the meantime, you –

CHRIS

Couldn't you do the exorcism yourself?

KARRAS

Look, every priest has the power to exorcise, but he has to have Church approval, and frankly, it's rarely ever given, so –

CHRIS

Can't you even *look* at her?

KARRAS

Well, as a psychiatrist, yes, I could, but –

CHRIS

She needs a *priest*! I've taken her to every goddamn fucking doctor psychiatrist in the world and they sent me to *you*! Now you send me to *them*?

KARRAS

But your –

CHRIS
(shrieking)
Jesus *Christ*, won't somebody *help her*!

She crumples against Karras's chest, moaning, with convulsive sobs.

Help her! Help her! Oh, somebody . . .

The final 'help' elides into deep, throaty sobbing.

INT. MACNEIL HOUSE STAIRCASE. DAY

Chris and Karras are ascending the staircase, Karras frowning in consternation at the off-screen sound, from Regan's bedroom, of the demonic voice threatening and raging. When they reach the door to Regan's bedroom, we pick up Karl leaning against the opposite wall, arms folded, head bowed.

KARL

It wants no straps, still.

Karras stares at him; looks at door; exchanges looks with Chris. Then he grasps the doorknob and starts to open the door. He reacts, as if to a noxious odor; then steels himself.

INT. REGAN'S BEDROOM. DAY

Close shot on door. Karras.

He enters, scanning the room; then he freezes, seeing:

POV: On bed – Regan. Arms held down by a double set of restraining straps, it seems no longer entirely Regan but something somehow demonic that now lies on the bed and turns its head to stare at the camera. The

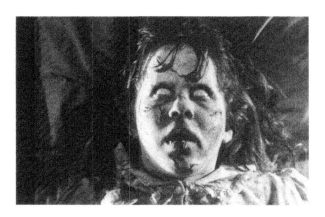

eyes bulge wide in wasted sockets, shining with a mad and burning intelligence. The hair is tangled and thickly matted, the legs and arms spider-thin, a distended stomach jutting up grotesquely. Her face is puffy, scratched and bruised from self-mutilation. In that husky voice:

REGAN/DEMON

So it's you. After all, they sent you.

The Regan/Demon entity throws back its head and roars with yelping, spine-chilling laughter. Karras is momentarily taken aback. Then, reining in his revulsion, he slowly and warily closes the door behind him and we follow closely as he fetches a chair to the bedside.

KARRAS

Hello, Regan. I'm Damien Karras. I'm a friend of your mother's and I've come here to help you.

REGAN/DEMON

Well, then kindly have the goodness to undo these straps.

KARRAS

I'm afraid you might hurt yourself, Regan.

REGAN/DEMON

I'm not Regan.

KARRAS

Then who are you?

REGAN/DEMON

I'm the Devil.

KARRAS

Is that so?

REGAN/DEMON

Oh, I assure you.

KARRAS

Well, then why don't you just make the straps disappear?

REGAN/DEMON

That's much too vulgar a display of power, Karras. Too crude. After all, I'm a prince.

KARRAS

But you won't give me proof.

REGAN/DEMON

Parlor magic? Saw the Devil in half?

KARRAS

Just make the straps disappear.

REGAN/DEMON

It's unworthy. And besides, it would deprive you of the opportunity of performing a charitable act.

KARRAS

Then let's try a different test. Let's test your knowledge.

REGAN/DEMON

How bizarre.

KARRAS

If you're the Devil, you know everything, right?

REGAN/DEMON

No, not quite. *Almost* everything. There. They say I'm proud. As you can see, I am not.

KARRAS

Let's try a question. Where is Regan?

REGAN/DEMON

In here. With us.

KARRAS

Who is 'us'?

REGAN/DEMON

Loose the straps. I can't talk. I'm accustomed to gesturing. I spend most of my time in Rome. In the meantime, I've passed your preposterous test.

KARRAS

Yes, if Regan's really in there.

REGAN/DEMON

Oh, she is.

KARRAS

Then let me see her.

REGAN/DEMON

Very sly. Put her back in control and push me out, is that it?

KARRAS

Oh, well, it's clear you're not the Devil.

REGAN/DEMON

Who said that I was?

KARRAS

Well, didn't you?

REGAN/DEMON

I don't know. Perhaps I did. I'm not sure. I'm not well.

KARRAS

Christ drove demons out of people, not the Devil.

REGAN/DEMON

Ah, that's it, then. Yes, of course. It makes sense. I'm a demon.

KARRAS

Which one?

REGAN/DEMON

(*ominous*)

I do not think you'd want to know that, Priest.

KARRAS

Priest?

Karras starts to say something else, then abruptly half-turns his head as if reacting to an invisible, chilling force at the back of his neck.

REGAN/DEMON

Yes, Karras. Icy fingers at the back of your neck? And now colder? Gripping tighter . . . tighter . . . ?

Karras jerks out of an apparently hypnotic state. The Demon laughs.

Yes, of course, Karras. Autosuggestion. Whatever would we do without the unconscious mind?

KARRAS

(*now wary; uneasy*)

Who are you? What's your name?

REGAN/DEMON

Call us 'Legion', Karras. We are many. A little gathering of poor lost homeless souls.

KARRAS

What's your reason for coming into Regan?

REGAN/DEMON

Ah, yes, that's the mystery, isn't it?

KARRAS

How long are you planning to stay?

REGAN/DEMON

How long? Until she rots and lies stinking in the earth! Until the worms have curled festering garlands in her hair and come crawling through the pus-oozing sockets of her eyes, the little – !

The Demon breaks off, trembling with rage; then falls back on the bed.

There, you see how these straps have upset me, Karras? Take them off.

KARRAS

Well, as I said, I'll con–

Abruptly, Karras breaks off, transfixed upon seeing:

Karras's POV: Push to close angle on Regan. The features more authentically Regan's, her eyes filled with terror, her mouth gaping open in an electrifying shriek of agony that is simulated by a piercing stab of the dramatic score. A succession of different personalities, beings – including Dennings – flash across her countenance.

Close on Karras reacting. He bends head, pinches bridge of nose, as if shaking off a visual illusion. The shriek ends and now we hear the voice of the Derelict in the subway station:

DERELICT
(*voice-over*)

Couldya help an old altar boy, Faddah? I'm a Cat'lic.

Then mocking laughter as Karras looks up in wonder.

Back to scene.

REGAN/DEMON

Incidentally, your mother's in here with us, Karras. Would you like to leave a message? I'll see that she gets it.

The Demon laughs.

KARRAS
(*hooked; a pause before*)

If that's true, then you must know my mother's maiden name.

Regan nods, emitting a teasing groan of assent.

What is it?

Regan shakes her head, her eyes closed, and she lies back with a long and rattling exhalation of breath.

What is it?

Regan's lips begin to move, and she whispers something over and over, a single word we cannot make out. Karras slowly leans his head down close, his ear to her mouth trying to make it out. And suddenly jerks

105

away with a cry as from Regan's mouth there erupts a deafening, angry bellowing, as of an alien steer, that shivers through the walls of the room.

On Regan still bellowing, her eyes roll up in her sockets, exposing the whites. Her neck grows elongated, an enormous goiter bulging in it.

INT. CHRIS'S BATHROOM AND HALL OFF BEDROOM. LATE DAY

Karras's sweater is draped over the shower pole as he washes his hands at the sink. Chris sits on the edge of the tub, anxiously fidgeting with a towel in her lap as she watches Karras. From down the hall, off-screen, we hear varied animal sounds.

> KARRAS
> But your daughter doesn't say she's a demon, Miss MacNeil, she says she's the Devil himself and if you've seen as many psychotics as I have, you'd know that's like saying you're Napoleon Bonaparte.

> CHRIS
> Look, I'll tell you something, Father. You show me Regan's identical twin: same face, same voice, same smell, same everything down to the way she dots her 'i's, and still I'd know in a second that it wasn't really her! I'd know it! I'd know it in my gut and I'm telling you that thing up there is not my daughter!
>> (*she leans back, drained*)
> Now you tell me what to do. Go ahead: you tell me that you know for a *fact* there's nothing wrong with my daughter except in her head; that you know for a *fact* that she doesn't need an exorcism; that you know it wouldn't do her any good. Go ahead! You tell me! You tell me that!

For long troubled seconds, the priest is still. Then he answers softly:

> KARRAS
> Well, there's little in this world that I know for a fact.

Chris stares at him a brief beat, then rises and moves quickly out of the bathroom. Karras frowns, hearing Regan howling like a wolf. Chris returns with a framed photo of Regan and shows it to him.

CHRIS

That's her. That's Regan. That was taken four months ago.

Karras is deeply affected.

KARRAS

Look, I'm only against the chance of doing your daughter
more harm than good.

CHRIS

But you're talking now strictly as a psychiatrist, right?

KARRAS

No, I'm talking now also as a priest. If I go to the Chancery
office to get permission to perform an exorcism, the first thing
I'd have to have is a pretty substantial indication that your
daughter's condition isn't a purely psychiatric problem. After
that, I'd need evidence the Church would accept as signs of
possession.

CHRIS

Like what?

KARRAS

Well, like her speaking in a language that she's never known
or studied.

CHRIS

And what else?

KARRAS

I don't know. I'm going to have to look it up.

CHRIS

I thought you were supposed to be an expert.

KARRAS

There *are* no experts. You probably know more about
demonic possession right now than most priests.

EXT. MACNEIL HOUSE. NIGHT

*Chris opens the door for Karras. He steps out on to the stoop carrying
the witchcraft book and a slender box containing a tape-recording.*

107

KARRAS

Did your daughter know a priest was coming over?

CHRIS

No. No, nobody knew but me.

KARRAS

Did you know that my mother had died just recently?

CHRIS

Yes, I'm very sorry.

KARRAS

Is Regan aware of it?

CHRIS

Why?

KARRAS

Is she aware of it?

CHRIS

No, not at all.

Karras nods.

Why'd you ask?

KARRAS
(*shrugging*)

Not important. I just wondered.

He studies Chris for a moment without expression, then quickly moves away. Chris watches from the doorway. Karras crosses the street. At the corner, he drops the book and stoops quickly to retrieve it, then rounds the corner and vanishes from sight. Chris closes the door. And now the camera discloses Kinderman observing the house from an unmarked car parked a little down the street, toward the campus library.

EXT. PROSPECT STREET. NIGHT

Kinderman frowns in puzzlement as he sees something: in the window of Regan's bedroom (the shutters are partially open), a suggestion of a slender figure (Regan?) quickly ducking away from sight. We go back to Kinderman, thoughtful. He does not see the shutter slowly pulled shut.

108

EXT. GEORGETOWN UNIVERSITY CAMPUS. NIGHT

Low ground fog. We hear a soft, low, eerie wind.

INT. UNIVERSITY LIBRARY. NIGHT

Karras is alone, seated at a small table in an alcove on the lower floor. A single reading lamp is the sole illumination. The table now has several books stacked on it. He is reading from one of them:

KARRAS

(voice-over)

'Of the four Jesuit exorcists sent to deal with an outbreak of demonic possession at the Ursuline Convent in Loudon, France, three – Fathers Lucas, Lactance and Tranquille – not only became possessed themselves but also died while in that state of either shock or cardiac exhaustion. The fourth exorcist, Father Surin, whose age was only twenty-eight and who was France's foremost intellectual –

(a beat as Karras absorbs what's next)

– became insane and so remained for the last thirty years of his life.

A beat. Then from somewhere in the library an odd, slow creaking sound, like a surreptitious footfall, is heard. Karras looks up warily. He sees nothing.

INT. GEORGETOWN UNIVERSITY JESUIT RESIDENCE HALL. NIGHT

Karras comes toward us, knocks on a door.

KARRAS

Hey, Joe, pal?

From within we hear a chair sliding, then footsteps. Dyer opens the door.

DYER

You wish to make your confession, my son?

KARRAS

I need a tape-recorder, Joe. A cassette player. Think you can get me one?

                              DYER
                    (*holding out his hand, palm up*)
    Lemon drop.

And as Karras shakes his head ruefully and reaches into a pocket:

    Make it two. You want to shake your head some more? We'll
    make it three.

EXT. GEORGETOWN CAMPUS. KARRAS'S WINDOW. NIGHT

*Through the window, we see Karras hunched over a tape-recorder on
his desk. He wears stereo earphones.*

INT. KARRAS'S ROOM. NIGHT

The tape-recorder is running and we hear:

                             REGAN
                          (*voice-over*)
    Hello . . .

Whining feedback. Then:

                             CHRIS
                          (*voice-over*)
    Not so close to the microphone, honey. Hold it back.

                             REGAN
                          (*voice-over*)
    Like this?

                             CHRIS
                          (*voice-over*)
    No, more.

                             REGAN
                          (*voice-over*)
    Like this?
                       (*muffled giggling; then*)
    Hello, Daddy? This is me.
                    (*giggling; then a whispered aside*)
    I can't tell what to say.

CHRIS

(*voice-over*)

Oh, just tell him how you are, Rags, and what you've been doin'.

Karras looks more and more shaken as he listens.

REGAN

(*voice-over*)

Ummm, Daddy – well, ya see; I mean I hope you can hear me okay and – let's see. Umm, well, first we're – No, wait, now . . . See, first we're in Washington, Daddy, ya know? It's – No, wait, now, I better start over.

INT. CUBICLE. DAY

On Karras. In a tiny room used by the Jesuits for the saying of their daily Mass. Standing at the altar, informally dressed, Karras lifts the communion host in consecration.

KARRAS

'Then he broke the bread, blessed it, gave it to his disciples, and said: "Take this, all of you, and eat it. For this – is – My body."'

His fingers, holding the host, tremble with a hope he dares not hope: that the words he has just spoken might be literally true.

INT. REGAN'S BEDROOM. DAY

Close on tape-recorder. A full reel is just beginning to wind on to an empty reel. A microphone is propped in position. Karras sits at the foot of the bed. He is in his clerical robes.

REGAN/DEMON

Hello, Karras. What an excellent day for an exorcism. Do begin it soon.

KARRAS

(*puzzled*)

You would like that?

REGAN/DEMON

Intensely.

KARRAS

But wouldn't that drive you out of Regan?

REGAN/DEMON

It would bring us together.

KARRAS

You and Regan?

REGAN/DEMON

You and us.

Karras stares and then reacts as he feels something cold and unseen at his neck. Then he jerks his head around at a loud, sudden banging sound. Off-screen a bureau drawer has popped open, sliding out its entire length. The Demon bursts into hysterical, gleeful laughter.

KARRAS

You did that?

REGAN/DEMON

Assuredly.

KARRAS

Do it again.

REGAN/DEMON

In time, in time. But *mirabile dictu*, don't you agree?

KARRAS
(*startled*)

You speak Latin?

REGAN/DEMON

Ego te absolvo.

The Demon chuckles.

KARRAS
(*excitedly*)

Quod nomen mihi est?

REGAN/DEMON

Bon jour.

KARRAS
(persistent)

Quod nomen mihi est?

REGAN/DEMON

Bon nuit. La plume de ma tante.

The Demon laughs full and mockingly. Karras holds up a small vial of water that he has had cupped in his hand. The Demon abruptly breaks off the laughter.

(warily)

What is that?

KARRAS

Holy water.

Karras has uncapped the vial and now sprinkles its contents over Regan. Instantly, Regan/Demon writhes to avoid the spray, howling in pain and terror.

REGAN/DEMON

Ahhhhhhhhhhhh! It burns me! It burns! It burns! Ah, cease, priest, bastard! Cease! Ahhhhhhhh!

Karras looks disappointed. The howling ceases and Regan's head falls back on to the pillow. Regan's eyes roll upward into their sockets, exposing the whites. Regan/Demon is now rolling her head feverishly from side to side muttering an indistinct gibberish:

I'drehtellteeson. Dobetni tee siti. Leafy. Tseerpet reef. Emitsuvig.

Karras is intrigued and moves to the side of the bed. He turns up the volume on the recorder, then lowers his ear to Regan's mouth to pick it up. He listens. The gibberish ceases and is replaced by deep and raspy breathing. Karras straightens up.

KARRAS

Who are you?

REGAN/DEMON

Nowonmai . . . Nowonami . . .

KARRAS

Is that your name?

The lips move. Fevered syllables, slow and unintelligible. Then it ceases.

Are you able to understand me?

Silence. Only the eerie sound of breathing. Karras waits a little; then he shakes his head, disappointed. He grips Regan's wrist to check her pulse; then he draws back Regan's nightgown top and looks with a pained expression at the sight of her skeletal ribs. He shakes his head.

INT. MACNEIL HOUSE. STUDY. DAY

Chris is at the bar. Karras enters.

KARRAS

I'm not hopeful I could ever get permission from the Bishop.

CHRIS

Why *not?*

He holds up the empty vial.

KARRAS

I just told her this was holy water; when I sprinkled it on her, she reacted very violently.

CHRIS

And so?

KARRAS

It's just ordinary tap water.

CHRIS

Christ, who *gives* a shit! She's *dying!*

KARRAS

Where's her father?

CHRIS

In Europe.

114

KARRAS

Have you told him what's happening?

CHRIS

No!

KARRAS

Well, I think it would help if he were here. It's –

CHRIS

(*over him*)

I've asked you to drive a demon *out*, goddamnit, not ask another one *in*! What the hell good is *Howard* right now? What's the *good*?

KARRAS

There's a strong possibility that Regan's disorder is caused by her guilt over –

CHRIS

(*hysterical*)

Guilt over *what*?

KARRAS

It could –

CHRIS

Over the divorce? All that psychiatric bullshit?

KARRAS

It's –

CHRIS

She's guilty 'cause she killed Burke Dennings! She killed him!

INT. LANGUAGE LAB. NIGHT

Karras and the language lab director, Frank, are listening to the tail-end of the recording of Karras's last session with Regan. Karras is tense.

KARRAS

Well, all right, is it a language or not?

FRANK

Oh, I'd say it was a language all right. It's English.

KARRAS

It's *what?*

Frank is threading another tape on to the recorder.

FRANK

I thought you were putting me on. It's just English in reverse.
I've pulled your questions, flipped the responses, and
respliced them in sequence.
(*pushing playback button*)
Here, you just play it backwards.

INT. KARRAS'S ROOM. NIGHT

*Karras sits in front of the tape-recorder listening to an eerie, unearthly
series of various whispered voices.*

FIRST VOICE
(*on tape-recorder*)

Let her die!

SECOND VOICE
(*on tape-recorder*)
No, no, sweet! It is sweet in the body! I feel!

THIRD VOICE
(*on tape-recorder*)

Fear the priest.

SECOND VOICE
(*on tape-recorder*)

Give us time.

THIRD VOICE
(*on tape-recorder*)

He is ill.

FOURTH VOICE
No, not this one. The other. The one who will –

SECOND VOICE
(*on tape-recorder; interrupting*)
Ah, the blood! Feel the blood! How it sings!

KARRAS'S VOICE
(*on tape-recorder*)

Who are you?

FIRST VOICE
(*on tape-recorder*)

I am no one.

KARRAS'S VOICE
(*on tape-recorder*)

Is that your name?

SECOND VOICE
(*on tape-recorder*)

I have no name.

FIRST VOICE
(*on tape-recorder*)

I am no one.

THIRD VOICE
(*on tape-recorder*)

Many.

FOURTH VOICE
(*on tape-recorder*)

Let us be. Let us warm in the body.

SECOND VOICE
(*on tape-recorder*)

Leave us.

THIRD VOICE
(*on tape-recorder*)

Let us be, Karras.

FIRST VOICE
(*on tape-recorder*)

Merrin . . . Merrin.

Phone rings. Karras leaps for it.

KARRAS

(*urgently*)

Hello, yes? . . . Be right over.

EXT. PROSPECT STREET. NEAR THE HOUSE. NIGHT

Very late. No traffic noise. Karras is hastily crossing, throwing on a sweater.

INT. ENTRY OF MACNEIL HOUSE. NIGHT

Sharon, wearing a sweater and holding a flashlight, has the door open, waiting as Karras comes up the steps. At the door, she puts a finger to her lips for quiet. She beckons him in and closes the door silently and carefully.

SHARON

(*whispering*)

I don't want to wake Chris. I don't think she ought to see this.

She beckons Karras to follow.

INT. SECOND-FLOOR HALL BY REGAN'S DOOR. NIGHT

The house is darkened. Karras and Sharon are silently approaching. Sharon carefully opens the door, enters, and beckons Karras into the room.

INT. REGAN'S BEDROOM AT DOOR. NIGHT

As he enters and Sharon closes the door, Karras reacts as if to extreme cold. His breath, like Sharon's, is frostily condensing in the chill air of the room. He looks at Sharon with wonder.

Another angle as Karras and Sharon approach the bedside. The room is dark except for a night-light glow. Sharon has the flashlight on now, trained low. They stop by the bed. Regan seems to be in a coma, the whites of her eyes glowing eerily in the dim light. Heavy breathing. Karras takes her wrist to check her pulse. The naso-gastric tube is in place, Sustagen seeping into Regan's motionless body. Beads of perspiration on Regan's forehead. Sharon is bending, gently pulling

Regan's pajama tops wide apart, exposing her chest. Karras wipes a little perspiration off Regan's forehead, then stares at it on his fingers, rubbing them together with deeper consternation. Then he looks up at Sharon, feeling her gaze upon him.

SHARON

(whispering)

I don't know if it's stopped. But watch. Just keep looking at her chest.

Karras follows her instruction. One beat. Two. Then, flipping flashlight beam on to Regan's chest:

(whispering)

There! There, it's coming!

Karras leans his face closer to observe, then halts, shocked at:

POV: Regan's chest. Rising up slowly on her skin in blood-red, bas-relief script are two words: HELP ME.

Close on Sharon and Karras reacting.

INT. HEALY BUILDING. GROUND-FLOOR HALLWAY. DAY

Karras walks down the hallway toward the stairs.

INT. HEALY BUILDING MAIN STAIRWAY. DAY

Karras climbs stairs and enters Cardinal's outer office.

INT. CARDINAL'S OFFICE. DAY

In the room, Karras and the Cardinal.

CARDINAL

You're convinced that it's genuine.

Karras looks down, thinking for a moment.

KARRAS

I don't know. No, not really. But I've made a prudent judgment that it meets the conditions set forth in the Ritual.

CARDINAL

You would want to do the exorcism yourself?

Karras nods.

How's your health?

KARRAS

All right.

CARDINAL

Well, we'll see. It might be best to have a man with
experience. Maybe someone who's spent time in the foreign
missions. Let's see who's around. In the meantime I'll call
you as soon as I know.

INT. GEORGETOWN UNIVERSITY PRESIDENT'S OFFICE. DAY

PRESIDENT

Well, he does know the background. I doubt there's any
danger in just having him assist. There should be a
psychiatrist present, anyway.

CARDINAL

And what about the exorcist? Any ideas? I'm blank.

PRESIDENT

Well, now, Lankester Merrin's around.

CARDINAL

Merrin? I had a notion he was over in Iraq. I think I read he
was working on a dig around Nineveh.

PRESIDENT

That's right. But he finished and came back around three or
four months ago, Mike. He's at Woodstock.

CARDINAL

What's he doing there? Teaching?

PRESIDENT

No, he's working on another book.

CARDINAL

Don't you think he's too old, though, Tom? How's his health?

PRESIDENT

Well, it must be all right or he wouldn't be running around digging up tombs, don't you think?

CARDINAL

Yes, I guess so.

PRESIDENT

And besides, he's had experience, Mike.

CARDINAL

I didn't know that.

PRESIDENT

Maybe ten or twelve years ago, I think, in Africa. Supposedly the exorcism lasted for months. I heard it damn near killed him.

EXT. PROSPECT STREET IN FRONT OF MACNEIL HOUSE. NIGHT

A cab pulls up to the house in long shot. Out of the cab steps a tall, old priest (Merrin), carrying a battered valise. A hat obscures his face. As the cab pulls away, Merrin stands rooted, staring up at the second floor of the MacNeil house like a melancholy traveler frozen in time.

INT. REGAN'S BEDROOM. NIGHT

Regan is apparently unconscious, her features recomposed into her own in the normal state (as happens whenever she's unconscious). Sharon is winding sphygmomanometer wrappings around Regan's arm while Karras pinches Regan's Achilles tendon, checking her sensitivity to pain. During this:

SHARON

Four hundred milligrams in less than two hours! That's enough to put an *army* out!

Karras nods; silently takes Regan's blood pressure.

KARRAS

Ninety over sixty.

INT. ENTRY TO MACNEIL HOUSE. NIGHT

Chris opens the door, disclosing Merrin, face still shaded by the hat, and Roman collar by coat buttoned at the top.

CHRIS

Yes?

MERRIN
(reaching for hat)
Mrs MacNeil? I'm Father Merrin.

And now we see it is the Old Man in khaki from the opening sequence.

CHRIS
(flustered)
Oh, my gosh, please come in! Oh, come *in*!

Suddenly, Chris flinches at a sound from above: the voice of the Demon, booming, yet muffled, like amplified premature burial.

REGAN/DEMON
(off-screen)

Merriiiinnnnnnnnn!

CHRIS

God almighty!

REGAN/DEMON
(off-screen)

Merriiinnnnnnn!

Karl steps, incredulous, from the study and Karras comes out from the kitchen. Merrin turns and puts a hand out to Karras.

MERRIN
(warmly; serene)

Father Karras.

KARRAS
Hello, Father. Such an honor to meet you.

Merrin takes Karras's hand in both of his, searching Karras's face with a look of gravity and concern while upstairs the demonic laughter segues into vicious obscenities directed at Merrin.

MERRIN

Are you tired?

KARRAS

No, Father.

MERRIN

I should like you to go quickly across to the residence and gather up a cassock for myself, two surplices, a purple stole, some holy water, and your copy of *The Roman Ritual*. The large one. I believe we should begin.

KARRAS

Don't you want to hear the background of the case, first?

MERRIN

Why?

EXT. RESIDENCE HALL AREA. NIGHT

Karras, in his cassock, is crossing swiftly toward the house carrying a cardboard laundry box.

123

EXT. MACNEIL HOUSE. NIGHT

Karras enters.

INT. MACNEIL HOUSE. STUDY. NIGHT

Karras and Merrin are dressing in vestments taken out of the laundry box.

MERRIN

Especially important is the warning to avoid conversations with the demon. We may ask what is relevant, but anything beyond that is dangerous. Extremely. Especially, do not listen to anything he says. The demon is a liar. He will lie to confuse us, but he will also mix lies with the truth to attack us. The attack is psychological, Damien. And powerful. Do not listen. Remember that. Do not listen.
(*as Karras hands him his surplice*)
Is there anything at all you would like to ask now?

KARRAS

No. But I think that it might be helpful if I gave you some background on the different personalities that Regan has manifested. So far, I'd say there seem to be three.

MERRIN

There is only one.

INT. SECOND-FLOOR LANDING, AT STAIRS. NIGHT

Merrin and Karras, fully vested, Roman Rituals *in their hands, slowly come to the stairs and ascend in single file, Karras after Merrin.*

Angle down hall from outside room as the priests approach. Chris and Sharon, bundled in sweaters, watch them. The priests halt by them; look at them a moment, then:

MERRIN

What is your daughter's middle name?

CHRIS

Theresa.

MERRIN

What a lovely name.

He nods; then looks to the door. The others follow suit.

(*continuing; nods to Karras*)

All right.

Karras opens the door, disclosing Karl sitting in a corner wearing a heavy hunting jacket, a look of bewilderment and fear on his face as he looks toward us. Merrin hangs motionless for a moment.

INT. REGAN'S BEDROOM. NIGHT

Merrin, just outside the door, staring in at:

Regan/Demon lifting head from pillow, staring at Merrin with burning eyes.

Another angle as Merrin steps into the room, followed by Karras, Chris and Sharon. Karras sees door is open, closes it. Merrin goes to side of bed while Karras moves to its foot. They halt. (Note: The room is freezing. Breath is condensing throughout.) A beat. Regan licks a wolfish, blackened tongue across dried lips with a sound like parchment being smoothed over. Then:

REGAN/DEMON

Proud scum! This time you are going to lose!

Regan tilts back head and laughs gleefully. Merrin traces the sign of the cross above her, then repeats the gesture at Karras and Karl, and as he plucks the cap from the holy water vial in his hand, the demonic laughter breaks off. Merrin begins sprinkling the holy water on Regan, and she jerks her head up, mouth and neck muscles trembling as she bellows inchoately with hatred and fury. Then:

MERRIN

Be silent!

The words have flung forth like bolts. Karras has flinched and jerked his head around in wonder at Merrin, who stares commandingly at Regan. The Demon is silent, returning his stare with eyes now hesitant, blinking and wary. Merrin caps the holy water vial routinely and

returns it to Karras, who slips it in his pocket and watches as Merrin kneels down beside the bed and closes his eyes in murmured prayer:

'Our Father, who art in . . .'

Regan spits and hits Merrin in the face with a yellowish glob of mucus that oozes slowly down the exorcist's cheek. His head still bowed, Merrin plucks a handkerchief out of his pocket and serenely, unhurriedly wipes away the spittle as:

'. . . heaven, hallowed be Thy name. Thy kingdom come, Thy will be done, on earth, as it is in heaven. Give us this day, our daily bread, and forgive us our trespasses, as we forgive those who trespass against us. And lead us not into temptation.'

KARRAS

'And deliver us from the evil one.'

Karras briefly looks up. Regan's eyes are rolling upwards into their sockets until only the whites are exposed. Karras looks uneasy, then returns to his text to follow as Merrin now stands, praying reverently:

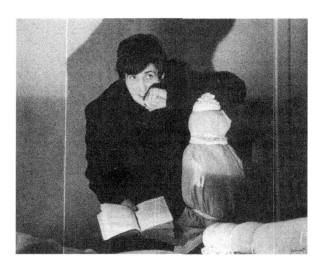

MERRIN

'God and Father of our Lord Jesus Christ, I appeal to your
holy name, humbly begging your kindness, that you may
graciously grant me help against this unclean spirit now
tormenting this creature of yours; through Christ our Lord.'

KARRAS

'Amen.'

*As Merrin continues reading, Karras again glances up as he hears
Regan hissing, sitting erect with the whites of her eyes exposed while her
tongue flicks in and out rapidly, her head weaving back and forth like a
cobra's. During this:*

MERRIN

'God, Creator and Defender of the human race, who made
man in your image, look down in pity on this your servant,
Regan Teresa MacNeil, now trapped in the coils of man's
ancient enemy, sworn foe of our race.'

After another look of disquiet, Karras looks down again to his text as:

'Save your servant.'

'Who trust in you, my God.'

'Let her find in you, Lord, a fortified tower.'

'In the face of the enemy.'

'Let the enemy have no power over her.'

On bed. The front legs are gently, rockingly rising up off the floor!

On Karl rising and hastily blessing himself.

On Chris.

On bed. It comes up jerkily, inches at a time, until the front legs are about a foot off the ground, at which point the back legs come up also. Then the bed hovers, bobbing and listing gently in the empty air as if floating on a stagnant lake, Regan still undulating and hissing.

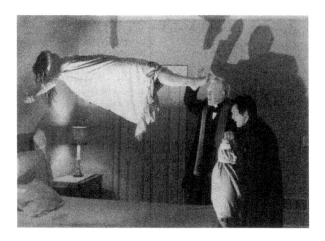

128

On Karras, transfixed.

(off-screen, gently)

Father Karras.

Karras doesn't hear it. A beat.

Damien.

Karras turns to Merrin. We see him eyeing Karras serenely as he motions with his head at the copy of the Ritual in Karras's hands.

The response, please, Damien.

Karras, still dumbfounded, glances again to the bed. Then he collects himself and looks down at his text.

KARRAS
(excited)

'And the son of iniquity be powerless to harm her.'

MERRIN

'Lord, hear my prayer.'

KARRAS

'And let my cry come unto Thee.'

Here Merrin reaches up his hand in a workaday manner and traces the sign of the cross unhurriedly three times on Regan's brow while:

MERRIN
(continuing to read aloud)

'. . . Almighty Father, everlasting God, who sent your only begotten Son into the world to crush that roaring lion . . .'

The hissing ceases and from the taut-stretched 'O' of Regan's mouth comes the nerve-shredding lowing of a steer, growing shatteringly louder and louder as:

'. . . snatch from ruination and from the clutches of the noonday devil this human being made in your image.'

Merrin reaches his hand up again (still reading aloud) and presses a portion of his purple stole to Regan's neck. Abruptly, the bellowing ceases and in the ringing silence a thick and putrid greenish vomit begins to pump from Regan's mouth in slow and regular, sickening spurts that

ooze like lava over her lip and flow in waves on to Merrin's hand,
which he does not move as we now hear:

> 'God and Lord of all creation, by whose might Satan was
> made to fall from heaven like lightning, strike terror into the
> beast now laying waste your vineyard. Let your mighty hand
> cast out this cruel demon from this creature. Drive out this
> persecutor of the innocent . . .'

The bed begins to rock lazily, and then to pitch, and then suddenly is
violently dipping and yawing. During this, the vomit is still pumping
from Regan's mouth and Merrin routinely makes adjustments, keeping
the stole firmly to Regan's neck.

During the latter part of the prayer, the bed has ceased its movements
and floated with a cushioned thud to the rug, and Karras now stares
mesmerized at Merrin's hand buried under the thick and mounded
vomit.

Damien?

Karras turns to him blankly.

> 'Lord, hear my prayer.'

KARRAS
(turning to the bed)
'And let my cry come unto Thee.'

Now Merrin takes a step back and jolts the room with the lash of his
voice as he commands:

MERRIN
'I cast you out, unclean spirit, along with every satanic power
of the enemy! Every specter from hell! Every savage
companion! It is Christ who commands you, He who flung
you headlong from the heights of Heaven! You robber of life!
You corrupter of justice! You inventor of every obscenity!'

As Merrin speaks, Regan ceases vomiting, Karras moves slowly around
to bedside and reaches down, checking Regan's pulse. She is silent and
unmoving. Into icy air, thin mists of vapor waft upward from the vomit
like a reeking offering. And now Karras lifts his eyes, staring, as with
nightmare slowness, a fraction at a time, Regan's head turns toward

*him, swiveling like a mannequin's and creaking with the sound of a
rusted mechanism until the dread and glaring whites of the eyes are fixed
directly on Karras. And now Karras glances up warily as the lights in
the room begin flickering, dimming, then fade to an eerie, pulsing
amber. Regan turns back toward Merrin, and now a muffled pounding
jolts the room; then another; and another, and then steadily, the
splintering sound of throbbing at a ponderous rate like the beating of a
heart that is massive and diseased.*

(*off-screen*)

'Why do you stand and resist, knowing as you must that
Christ the Lord brings your plans to nothing. He has already
stripped you of your powers and laid waste your kingdom. He
has cast you forth into the outer darkness. To what purpose
do you brazenly refuse? For you are guilty before almighty
God, whose laws you have transgressed. You are guilty before
His Son, our Lord Jesus Christ, whom you dared to nail to
the cross. You are guilty before the whole human race.'

(*oblivious*)

'Depart, you monster! Your place is in solitude! Your abode
is in a nest of vipers! Get down and crawl with them! It is
God Himself who commands you . . . '

131

Merrin continues and now the poundings begin to come steadily louder, faster, until Sharon cries out, pressing fists against her ears as the poundings grow deafening and now suddenly accelerate to a terrifying tempo. And then abruptly the poundings cease and Merrin's prayer comes through clear in the silence.

'Oh, God of heaven and earth, God of the angels and archangels . . .'

Over the continued recitation, we hear the return of the Demon as the flickering haze grows gradually brighter.

REGAN/DEMON	MERRIN
(raging at Merrin)	*(off screen)*
Hypocrites!	'God who has power to bestow life after death and rest after toil. I humbly entreat you to
Liar! Proud bastard! Go back to the mountain top and speak to your only equal!	deliver this servant of yours, Regan Teresa MacNeil, from the unclean spirit.'

On Merrin.

MERRIN

'I adjure you, ancient serpent, by the judge of the living and the dead, by your . . .'

Angle on Regan. As Merrin continues, off-screen, Regan begins to emit various animal noises, and Karras, a hypodermic syringe in one hand, moves to the bedside, nodding for Chris and Sharon to approach. As he does, the Dennings personality takes over in Regan, turning to plead with Karras:

REGAN/DENNINGS

Good Christ, Karras! What in thunderation are you *doing*? Can't you see the little bitch should be in hospital? She belongs in a madhouse! Now *really*! Let's stop all this mumbo-jumbo! If she dies, you know, it's *your* fault! Just because *he's* stubborn –

(indicating Merrin)

– doesn't mean *you* should behave like a snot! And anyway, it simply isn't fair to drive us out! I mean, speaking for myself, it's only justice I should be where I am. The little bitch! I was minding my business at the bar that night when I thought I heard the little slut moaning, so I went upstairs to see what was the matter – swear to God, it was for no other reason! *None!* – and she bloody well took me by my bloody ruddy throat! Christ, I've never in my *life* seen such strength! Screamed I'd diddled her mother or some such, and saying that I'd caused the divorce. It wasn't clear. But I tell you, love, she pushed me out the window! Yes, she did. Now you really think it's fair to chuck me out? You think it's –?

The entity breaks off, jerking her head toward Chris, as Chris and Sharon come to the bedside.

REGAN/DEMON
Ah, the mother of piglet! Yes, come see your handiwork, sow!

While Sharon and Chris pin Regan's arms, Karras administers the injection.

(to Chris)
See the puke! See the murderous bitch! Are you pleased! It is *you* who has done it! Yes, you with your career before her, before *husband*, before – !

KARRAS	REGAN/DEMON
(to Chris)	– anything! The *divorce* is the
All right, swab it! Swab the	cause of her illness! Go to
arms! Over here!	priests, will you! Priests will not
(as Chris moves)	help! She is mad! You have
And don't listen! Don't –!	driven her to madness and to
	murder! You have driven her
	into her grave! She – !

And now the Demon has jerked its head around to Karras, eyes bulging with fury.

REGAN/DEMON
And *you*, bastard! *You!*

Chris has swabbed Regan's arm and as Karras flicks the needle into wasted flesh:

KARRAS

(*to Chris*)

Now get out!

As Chris flees the room we are:

On Demon.

REGAN/DEMON

Yes, we *know* of your kindness to *mothers*!

On Karras. His head is lowered as he extracts the needle, and we hear the off-screen mocking laughter of the Demon. Karras blanches and for a moment does not move.

MERRIN

(*continuing adjuration*)

'The mystery of the Cross commands you! The faith of the saints and the martyrs commands you! The blood of Christ commands you! The prayers of – '

Merrin breaks off and looks up at hearing the Demon cry in sudden pain, as well as anger. He repeats the line that produced this effect:

'The blood of Christ commands you!'

Same reaction; greater.

'The blood of Christ commands you.'

Midway through the word 'command', however, a prolonged howl of pain and rage from:

REGAN/DEMON

Daaaammmmn youuuuu, Merrrriiinnnn!

But the cry of 'Merrin' gives way to a prolonged exhalation of breath, almost as in death. And now from Regan comes the slow, lilting singing – in a sweet clear voice like a choirboy's – of a hymn sung at Catholic benediction: 'Tantum Ergo'.

On Regan/Demon. The whites of the eyes are exposed. The singing.

A full angle on Regan, Karras as Merrin appears with a towel. He wipes the vomit from Regan's face with tender, weary movements. Sharon enters the room and comes to the bed. She takes the towel from Merrin's hands.

SHARON

I'll finish that, Father.

Karras checks Regan's pulse.

KARRAS
(*to Sharon*)
Clean her up, please, and give her half of a twenty-five
milligram Compazine suppository.

EXT. HALL OUTSIDE REGAN'S BEDROOM. NIGHT

*From within the bedroom we hear the sweet singing of another hymn:
'Panis Angelicus', and in the dimness, Merrin and Karras lean wearily
against the wall opposite the door to the room. Karras is staring at it.
Then, he begins a hesitant dialogue that will continue in hushed tones,
almost whispers:*

KARRAS

If it's possession, why her? Why this girl?

MERRIN

Who can know? Who can really hope to know. Yet I think –
the demon's target is not the possessed; it is us . . . the
observers . . . every person in this house. And I think – I think
the point is to make us despair, to reject our own humanity,
Damien, to see ourselves as ultimately bestial, as ultimately
vile and putrescent; without dignity, ugly and unworthy. And
there lies the heart of it, perhaps: in worthiness. For I think
belief in God is not a matter of reason at all; I think that it is
finally a matter of love: of accepting the possibility that God
could love *us.*

*Merrin looks up at the door and listens to the singing for a moment.
Then he continues:*

Yet even from this . . . from evil . . . will come good. In some
way. In some way that we may never understand or ever see.
Perhaps evil is the crucible of goodness . . . so that perhaps
even Satan . . . Satan, in spite of himself . . . somehow serves
to work out the will of God.

It has an impact. Karras thinks. Then:

KARRAS

Once the demon is driven out – what's to keep it from
coming back in?

MERRIN

I don't know. Yet it never seems to happen. Never.

He puts a hand to his face, tightly pinching at the corners of his eyes.

Damien . . . what a wonderful name.

*There is exhaustion in his voice. And something else, something like
repression of pain. Abruptly, Merrin pushes himself away from the wall,
and with his face still hidden in his hand:*

(*softly*)

Please excuse me.

*Merrin hurries down the hall out of sight of Karras, then takes out a pill
box, extracts a nitroglycerine tablet and places it under his tongue.
Karras turns to the door as Sharon emerges with a bundle of fouled
bedding and clothing. Karras takes a deep breath and enters.*

INT. REGAN'S BEDROOM. NIGHT

*Regan sleeps but Karras's frosty breath tells us the air in the room is still
icy. He shivers. Then he walks to the bedside, reaches down and grips
Regan's wrist to take her pulse. As he stares at the sweepsecond hand of
the wristwatch, we are close at Karras and we hear the voice of Karras's
Mother.*

REGAN/MOTHER

(*off-screen*)

You leave me to be priest, Dimmy. Send me institution.
Why? Why you do dis?

*Karras is almost trembling with the effort to keep from looking at
Regan's face. And now the voice grows frightened and tearfully
imploring.*

You always good boy, Dimmy. Please! I am 'fraid! Please
don't chase me outside, Dimmy! *Please!*

KARRAS
(*vehement whisper*)
You're not my mother!

REGAN/MOTHER

Dimmy, *please*!

KARRAS
You're not my – !

Intercut: Regan and Karras as the demonic entity now returns, raging:

REGAN/DEMON
Won't you face the truth! You believe what Merrin tells you?
You believe him to be holy? Well, he is not! And I will prove
it! I will prove it by killing the piglet!
(*grinning*)
Feel her pulse, Karras! Feel it!

Karras looks down at the wrist still gripped in his hand.

Somewhat rapid, Karras? Yes. But what else? As, yes, feeble.

As Karras leans quickly to his medical bag and extracts a stethoscope.

(*a laugh; then as Karras puts instrument to chest*)
Listen, Karras! Listen! Listen, well!

Karras looks very worried. Demon laughs. Then, as Merrin enters:

I will not let her sleep!

*The Demon puts its head back in prolonged, hideous laughter, Karras
staring numbly. Merrin comes to the bedside and looks at Regan, then
at Karras's stunned expression.*

MERRIN

What is it?

KARRAS
Her heart's begun to work inefficiently, Father. If she doesn't
get rest soon, she'll die from cardiac exhaustion.

MERRIN
(*alarmed*)
Can't you give her something? Drugs?

KARRAS

No, she might go into coma. If her blood pressure drops any more . . .

EXT. HOUSE ACROSS POTOMAC. SUNRISE

INT. REGAN'S BEDROOM. DAWN

Merrin is fighting sleep. Regan is grunting like a pig, whites of eyes exposed. Karras is checking Regan's heartbeat, and then her pulse, and then wraps black sphygmomanometer cloth around Regan's arm to take a blood-pressure reading. Both priests have blankets draped over their shoulders. Their breath is condensing in the frosty air of the room.

REGAN/MOTHER

I not good to you, Dimmy? Why you leave me to die all alone?

Merrin is at Karras's side, clutching at his arm and trying to draw him away, Karras resisting, his gaze fixed trancelike on the off-screen face.

MERRIN

Damien!

REGAN/MOTHER

Why, Dimmy?

MERRIN

Go and rest for a while!

On Regan. The features and eyes are subtly reminiscent of Karras's mother, but vividly evident is the large, circular mole that the mother had on her right cheek.

REGAN/MOTHER

Dimmy, *please*!

MERRIN

Go and rest!

Reluctantly, Karras leaves. Merrin, after a beat, turns to Regan. The demonic entity reappears.

REGAN/DEMON
(*seething whisper*)

You will lose!

INT. MACNEIL HOUSE. KITCHEN. LATE DAY

Chris is sitting at the breakfast nook looking at an album of photographs. She's on the verge of tears. Karras enters the kitchen, pauses as he sees Chris.

CHRIS
(*a sniffle*)

There's coffee there, Father.

Chris moves quickly past Karras with her face averted.

Excuse me.

She exits the kitchen. Karras's gaze shifts to the album. We see that these are candid photos of Regan. In one photograph, she is blowing out candles on a birthday cake. In another, she is sitting on a lake-front dock in shorts and T-shirt with 'Camp Brown Ledge' stencilled on the front. Karras is deeply affected. Close to a breakdown, he puts a trembling hand to brow, with a fervently whispered, desperate:

KARRAS

God . . . God help . . .

The camera follows him as he leaves the kitchen. Passing the living-room, he hears sobbing from within. Looking in, he sees Chris on the sofa convulsively weeping. Sharon, beside her, is comforting her.

INT. MACNEIL HOUSE. FOYER. LATE. DAY

Chris hears the front-door chimes. She reacts; waits. They ring again. She goes to answer. She opens the door, disclosing Kinderman.

KINDERMAN

I'm so sorry to dis–

He halts, eyeing her bruise. Chris knows what he's staring at. She puts a hand to the bruise. He stares for a beat. Then:

Look, I'm sorry to disturb you at this hour of the night, but

I'm afraid that I'm going to have to talk to your daughter, Mrs MacNeil, and I'd like to take a look at her room, if you don't mind.

CHRIS

Regan's bedroom?

KINDERMAN

Yes, immediately, please. I have a warrant.

CHRIS

Oh, please, not now! She's gotten worse, Lieutenant. Please! Please, not now!

INT. MACNEIL HOUSE. SECOND-FLOOR HALL. NIGHT

Karras enters Regan's bedroom and walks wearily to the chair where he had been sitting beside Merrin. During the above moves:

REGAN/DEMON
(off-screen)

. . . would have lost! Would have lost and you *knew* it, Merrin! *Bastard!*

Regan on bed. Merrin, limp and disjointed, lies sprawled face-down on floor on far side of bed and beside it. Regan/Demon cranes head over side of bed at him, croaking inchoately with rage and frustration.

Another angle as Karras rushes to Merrin, kneeling beside him, and turning him over, disclosing bluish coloration of Merrin's face.

(off-screen)

Die, will you? Die? Karras, heal him! Heal him! Bring him back that we may finishhhhhh ittttt!

And now inchoate croakings and moans of rage and frustration from off-screen, as Karras feels for Merrin's pulse and in a wrenching, stabbing instinct of anguish realizes that Merrin is dead.

KARRAS
(groaning in a whisper)

Ah, God no!

Karras sags back on his heels, an aching moan of grief rising up in his

throat as he shuts his eyes fiercely and shakes his head in despair. Then:

No!

Karras's eyes fix on something on the floor around Merrin: the pill box and a scattering of nitroglycerine pills. Karras begins gently and tenderly to place Merrin's hands on his chest in the form of a cross. An enormous, mucoid glob of yellowish spittle hits the dead man's eye.

On Regan/Demon.

> REGAN/DEMON
> (*mocking*)

The last rites!

Then it puts back its head and laughs long, and wildly, through:

> KARRAS

You son-of-a-bitch! You murdering bastard!

A projectile stream of vomit from off-screen strikes his face, but he is oblivious.

Yes, you're very good with children! Well, come on! Let's see you try something bigger!

Karras has his hands out like great fleshy hooks, beckoning, challenging.

Come on! Try me! Take *me*! Come into *me*!

On Regan/Demon. In the demonic features now, a trembling, wild-eyed rage; a fearsome struggle over some irresistibly tempting decision that the Demon is fighting against.

On Karras as he breaks off, his body jerking as if seized suddenly by some inner force alien to him. Yet his features do not change as his hands go to his throat and he struggles to his feet. His actions are those of a man who either has been possessed by or thinks he has been possessed by the Demon, but who also is fighting for control of his own organism. And now here, suddenly, on a move toward the bed and Regan (who, if she is in shot, is unconscious, her face in shadow), Karras's features briefly contort into those of the Demon Pazuzu, but then return to normal again on a backward jerk by Karras as:

No!

The Demon – in Karras's body – had moved to kill Regan; but Karras has won control now long enough to reach the window, rip the shutters off their hinges and leap out.

EXT. MACNEIL HOUSE. NIGHT

Karras hurtles out of the window.

Angle from near Regan's bedroom door as Chris, Sharon and Kinderman rush toward us.

INT. REGAN'S BEDROOM. NIGHT

Chris, Sharon and Kinderman burst in, halt. Sharon rushes forward toward window.

On Merrin as Chris rushes to him, kneels down by him, then reacts with shock.

CHRIS

Sharon! Come here! Quick, come – !

On Sharon and Kinderman staring down from the window. Hands to the sides of her face, Sharon is screaming.

POV: On Karras in street below.

Angle to include Chris and Kinderman as Sharon runs toward the door.

CHRIS

Shar, what is it!

SHARON
(*running out*)

Father Karras!

Chris rises and runs trembling toward the window.

On Chris and Kinderman from exterior window. Looking down, Chris freezes at what she sees. Then from behind her, in a small, wan voice calling tearfully:

REGAN
(*off-screen*)

Mother?

Chris half turns her head.

Mother, what's happening?

On Chris and Kinderman from interior room as they turn toward Regan.

(*off-screen*)
Oh, please! Please, come here!

On Regan. The real Regan, weeping in helpless confusion and fear.

Mother, please! I'm afraid!

Another angle as Chris rushes forward to Regan, arms outstretched, and weeping:

CHRIS
Rags! Oh, my baby, my baby!

She is on the bed and embracing her daughter.

EXT. 'HITCHCOCK' STEPS AREA ON 'M' STREET. NIGHT

Gathering of Passers-by at an accident scene. A Policeman shepherds them back. Dyer, followed by Sharon, is frantically pushing through as:

FIRST PASSER-BY

What happened?

SECOND PASSER-BY

Some guy fell down the steps.

POLICEMAN

Come on, now, move it back, folks. Give him air. Let him breathe.

Dyer has pushed through almost to the Policeman.

DYER

Let me through, please! Coming through! Coming – !

POV: On Karras. He lies crumpled and twisted in a pool of blood. Dyer kneels to him.

On Dyer and Karras. Low angle.

Damien . . . Can you talk?

Karras slowly and painfully reaches out his hand to Dyer's wrist and grips it, briefly squeezing. Fighting back the tears, Dyer leans his mouth close to Karras's ear.

Do you want to make your confession now, Damien?

Karras squeezes Dyer's wrist.

Are you sorry for all of the sins of your life and for having offended almighty God?

A squeeze. And now Dyer leans back and slowly traces the sign of the cross over Karras, reciting the words of absolution:

Ego te absolvo in nomine Patris, et Filii, et Spiritus Sancti. Amen.

On Dyer as he again leans over with his mouth close to Karras's ear.

Are you – ?

He halts, slightly turning his head towards his wrist.

Close on Dyer's wrist gripped by Karras. The grip slackens, the hand slowly opening, then falling limp.

Angle on Dyer and Karras. Slowly and tenderly, Dyer slips the eyelids down as we hear the wailing siren of an approaching ambulance. Dyer weeps . . .

SLOW FADE OUT:

FADE IN:

EXT. PROSPECT STREET FEATURING THE HOUSE. DAY

Full shot. Sharon exits the house carrying a suitcase which she places in the trunk of the limo parked in front of the house.

INT. MACNEIL HOUSE. SECOND-FLOOR HALL. DAY

Chris is coming toward Regan's bedroom.

CHRIS
(*calling*)

Hey, Rags, how ya comin'?

INT. REGAN'S BEDROOM. DAY

*Looking a little wan and gaunt, dark sacs beneath her eyes, Regan
stands by her bed, holding two stuffed animals in her grip as she stares
down with indecision and a child's discontent at an overpacked, open
suitcase.*

CHRIS

How ya comin', hon? We're late.

REGAN

There's just not enough *room* in this thing!

CHRIS

Well, ya can't take it all, now, sweetheart. Just leave it and
Willie'll bring it later on. Come on, babe, we've got to hurry
or we're going to miss the plane.

Doorchime sound.

REGAN
(*mildly pouting*)

Okay, okay.

CHRIS

That's my baby.

*Chris exits the scene, heading for the stairs. Regan sighs with
resignation, looking down at the animals.*

INT./EXT. MACNEIL HOUSE. FRONT-DOOR AREA. DAY

*Chris is opening the door, disclosing Dyer in cassock and Roman collar
saying goodbye to Sharon, the latter going to the limo at the curb and
getting in as Chris steps outside and:*

CHRIS

Oh, hi, Father.

DYER

Hi, Chris. Just came by to say 'so long'.

CHRIS

I was just about to call. We're just leaving.

DYER

Going to miss you.

CHRIS

Me too.

DYER

How's the girl?

CHRIS

Oh, she's great, really great.

Karl passes between them with two suitcases heading for Chris's car which is parked in front of house. Dyer nods a little glumly.

DYER

I'm glad.

CHRIS

She still can't remember.

DYER

Well, that's good.

CHRIS

Funny. He never even knew her.

Dyer looks up, and then so does Chris, their gazes meeting.

DYER

What do *you* think happened. Do you think she was really possessed?

CHRIS

Oh, yeah, you bet I do. I mean, if you're asking if I believe in the Devil, the answer is yes – yeah, that I believe.

DYER

But if all of the evil in the world makes you think that there might be a Devil – then how do you account for all of the good?

147

Chris's reaction reveals that this is a telling point. Then into the scene comes Regan, dressed to go.

                              REGAN

Okay, I finished.

                              CHRIS

Honey, this is Father Dyer.

                              REGAN

Hi, Father.

                              DYER

Hi.
                     (*tousles her hair*)

All set to go?

Regan has begun to stare oddly up at Dyer's Roman collar, some tugging remembrance in her eyes. Willie passes them with Regan's luggage, which she takes to the car to load in the trunk.

                              KARL

Ready, mizzes?

                              CHRIS

Okay, Karl.
                  (*taking Dyer's hand*)
Bye, Father. I'll call you from LA.

                              DYER

Goodbye, Chris.

Suddenly, impulsively, in a quick and unexpected move, Regan reaches up to Dyer, pulls his head down and kisses his cheek; a quick smack. Then, looking puzzled herself at what she has done:

                              REGAN

Goodbye.

                              DYER

Goodbye, dear.

Chris remembers the medal still in her hand. She offers it to him.

CHRIS

Oh, I forgot. Here.

Dyer, who instantly recognizes the medal, stares at it a moment. Then:

DYER

Why don't *you* keep it?

A beat. Dyer sees that Chris's eyes are clouding with tears.

It's all right, Chris. For him, it's the beginning.

Chris holds his gaze, then nods.

CHRIS

C'mon, Rags. Gotta hurry.

As Chris and Regan leave the frame, the camera stays on Dyer, turning to watch them. Then:

(*off-screen*)

Bye, Father!

POV: on car pulling away and moving quickly down Prospect Street.

On Dyer watching. Willie goes back inside the house. Off-screen sound of squeal of car brakes.

POV: on squad car. Kinderman is emerging, hurrying toward Dyer.

KINDERMAN

I came to say goodbye.

DYER

You just missed them.

Kinderman stops. A beat. Then:

KINDERMAN

How's the girl?

DYER

She seemed fine.

KINDERMAN

Ah, that's good. Very good. Well, that's all that's important. Back to business. Back to work. Bye now, Father.

He turns and takes a step toward the squad car, then stops and turns back to stare speculatively at Dyer.

You go to films, Father Dyer?

DYER

Sure.

KINDERMAN

I get passes.
(hesitates for a moment)
In fact, I've got a pass for the Crest tomorrow night. You'd like to go?

DYER

What's playing?

KINDERMAN

Wuthering Heights.

DYER

Who's in it?

KINDERMAN

Heathcliff, Jackie Gleason, and in the role of Catherine Earnshaw, Lucille Ball.

DYER

(expressionless)

I've seen it.

Kinderman stares limply for a moment, then looks away.

KINDERMAN
(murmuring)

Another one.

Then Kinderman steps up to the sidewalk, hooks an arm through Dyer's and slowly starts walking him down the street. Camera tracking front.

(fondly)
I'm reminded of a line in the film *Casablanca*. At the end Humphrey Bogart says to Claude Rains, 'Louie – I think this is the beginning of a beautiful friendship.'

Rear shot: Kinderman and Dyer.

DYER

You know, you *look* a little bit like Bogart.

KINDERMAN

You noticed.

The camera stays behind, but is rising. The street becomes busy as classes empty out at the university; students begin to appear in throngs, their laughter and chatter gradually growing as Kinderman mutely puts his arm around Dyer's shoulder and we:

FADE OUT.

The cast and crew for *The Exorcist* include:

CHRIS MACNEIL	Ellen Burstyn
FATHER MERRIN	Max von Sydow
LIEUTENANT KINDERMAN	Lee J. Cobb
FATHER KARRAS	Jason Miller
REGAN	Linda Blair
SHARON	Kitty Winn
BURKE DENNINGS	Jack MacGowran
FATHER DYER	Reverend William O'Malley, S.J.
DR KLEIN	Barton Heyman
CLINIC DIRECTOR	Peter Masterson
VOICE OF THE DEMON	Mercedes McCambridge

Costume Designer	Joseph Fretwell
Production Designer	Bill Malley
Set Decorator	Jerry Wunderlich
Sound	Chris Newman
Special Effects	Marcel Vercoutere
Make-up Artist	Dick Smith
Supervising Film Editor	J. Leondopoulos
Film Editors	Evan Lottman
	Norman Gay
Director of Photography	Owen Roizman
Director of Photography	
(Iraq Sequence)	Billy Williams
Associate Producer	David Salven
Executive Producer	Noel Marshall
Produced by	William Peter Blatty
Screenplay by	William Peter Blatty
	(based on his novel)
Directed by	William Friedkin

Printed in Great Britain
by Amazon